MW01280199

Soul Healing Forever

An Interactive Study Guide for Life Change in Christ

Tammy Smith, Ph.D.

ISBN: 978-0-615-33764-7

Printed in the United States of America
To order additional copies of this resource:
WRITE Threshold Counseling, 1115 Bethel Road, Columbus, OH 43220;
FAX order to (614) 451-3017; PHONE (614) 783-7821;
EMAIL tammy@onthethreshold.org; ONLINE at www.onthethreshold.org.

Special thanks to...

Wendy – Your unconditional, humble, faithful presence to serve as point for God's message through this work reflects your intimate, dedicated connection to Jesus. You completely bless me.

Carol – Your unwavering dedication to excellence through attention to detail is but a reflection of how you measure each minute of your life by Kingdom value. You amaze me.

Karen – Your passionate response to God's clear call for the healing of souls has been breathtaking to watch as you have stepped into your anointed appointment. You inspire me.

The Soul Healing Sisters of Faith – There aren't words enough to capture the depth of gratitude, awe, and joy for your partnership in this journey. Every minute has been unbelievable – and so much fun – so let's keep following! Your lives compel me to press on toward the goal.

CONTENTS

Soul Healing Forever
An Interactive Study Guide for Life Change in Christ

Dear Reader,

We are thrilled that you have decided to delve further into *Soul Healing* by engaging the Lord through this study guide. We are praying that God, who led you to this book, will speak to you as you work through its pages, seeking freedom and healing in Him.

Here are a few bits and pieces you might find useful before beginning:

The page numbers referenced throughout this study guide are based on the second edition of the *Soul Healing* book. If you have an earlier version, and the page numbers do not correspond, please accept our apologies. If you contact us about this, we will send you a second edition copy at the cost of only $6.99 (www.onthethreshold.org).

The questions found in each "Reflect" section of this guide follow the flow of the chapters in *Soul Healing*.

All Scripture references are from the NIV, unless otherwise noted.

Please go at your own pace through this study guide, taking time to process each section before moving on. This approach will give God time to use it to transform you. If you are working through this book in a group setting, we suggest that you break each chapter up into smaller sections in order to reap the most benefit from your effort. There are places in each chapter to pause, reflect, and spend some time praying or writing to the Lord about what He is doing within you. We realize that this might mean your group won't complete the entire study guide during a typical 12 or 16-week study. Moving at this slower pace will have its own benefits, because even the first several chapters alone provide a strong foundation for transformational healing and growth, and group members can complete the rest of the guide alone if necessary.

As you work through the book and study guide, you may find it helpful to keep a stack of index cards nearby. When God uses a specific verse or truth to impact you as you read, copy it onto an index card. You will hopefully collect quite a stack of verses throughout your journey of soul healing. Carry the stack of these truths with you in the car or your purse, or prop them up on your windowsill, or anywhere else that you will be sure to see them. This way, you will think more about them, and can even begin to memorize these life-changing nuggets of truth from God to you. The benefits of knowing Scripture are too numerous to count. You won't ever regret time spent on knowing God's Word.

I have hidden your word in my heart, that I might not sin against you.
Psalm 119:11

We are praying for your *Soul Healing* journey, and know that God Himself will meet you, instruct you, comfort you, and change you on every page, for He is a God who delights to reveal Himself to those who truly seek Him.

You will find me when you seek me with all your heart.
Jeremiah 29:13

Because of Jesus,

Tammy and the *Soul Healing* prayer team

Restoration

Imagine a rare painting. One with colors so vibrant, detail so intricate, and a scene so compelling that when you look at it, you can't take your eyes off it. The more you look at it, the more intriguing it becomes. In your eyes, it is pure beauty.

Imagine that same masterpiece, so rich and exquisite that it can't even be duplicated, under an inch of dust and grime, leaning on the ground behind a number of other paintings, in the back of someone's garage in a rural town.

That painting is you.

For we are God's masterpiece. He has created us anew in Christ Jesus, so we can do the good things he planned for us long ago.
Ephesians 2:10 (NLT)

You were made with unimaginable attention to detail: every aspect about you chosen with incomprehensible care, each hair on your head numbered, each day of your life selected, and each trait of yours intensely important. The compelling nature of your unique person is vaster than any natural wonder. It's probably almost laughable for you to think you are more amazing than the Grand Canyon. However, God would take issue with your smirking minimization. He says He set man over the works of His hands and knit each of us together, fearfully and wonderfully. (Ephesians 2:10, Matthew 10:30, Psalm 139:16, Psalm 8:4-6, Psalm 139:13-14)

For you created my inmost being; you knit me together in my mother's womb. I praise you because I am fearfully and wonderfully made; your works are wonderful, I know that full well.
Psalm 139:13-14

In short, you are His masterpiece.

"But look at me," you say. And it's very true – we are like that painting. We are hidden behind others. Even when pulled out into the open, we have dirty spots, areas where we've been soiled, and rips and tears seemingly everywhere. Life has been hard. People have hurt us, and we have come to believe garage life is easier than being on display. The thought of others beholding our intricacies, being captivated by our vibrancy, and ultimately, admiring the Mastermind behind the artistry seems inescapably far from reach.

Consider this study guide a special instrument designed to remove the masterpiece's residue from exposure to harsh elements. The result of its careful use will be a brilliant display of a Master Artist's intended work. The result will be restoration, expunging the years of neglect, misuse, and abandonment.

For we are God's workmanship created in Christ Jesus to do good works which God prepared in advance for us to do.
Ephesians 2:10 (NIV)

Introduction

Refresh

You may be wondering how we can so boldly assert that humans are mesmerizing works of art. After all, we are sinners. To our core, the Word says, we are self-interested. We walk straight into places that will mar the intended masterpiece, and we make choices which make the Monet seem like mud. (James 4:1-2, 2 Timothy 3:2, Philippians 2:21)

Yes, these tendencies are true. But there is a greater Truth that trumps the rest. It is quite literally the truth that changes everything. It is:

"I AM CRUCIFIED WITH CHRIST AND I NO LONGER LIVE, BUT CHRIST LIVES IN ME." Galatians 2:20

In other words, when we accept what Jesus did on the cross as the only means of salvation, we didn't add a new, heavenly nature to our old sinful one. We exchanged natures. It was quite literally His life for ours. (Isaiah 53:4-5, Matthew 8:17, 1 Peter 2:24) Salvation isn't just God forgiving our sins so we have an all-access pass to heaven when we die. Salvation is regeneration. It's a rebirth (thus the oft-used phrase "born again"). We are changed from sinner to saint. Because of Jesus' incredible work, the old person we were has been replaced by a new self, ruled by a new nature, one that was not there before (2 Corinthians 5:17).

Therefore, if anyone is in Christ, he is a new creation; the old has gone, the new has come!
2 Corinthians 5:17

The truth that changes everything is that our new self is the life of Jesus Christ implanted in us.

Ephesians 5:8 is vivid on this point: "You were formerly darkness, but now you are light in the Lord; walk as children of the light." Notice it doesn't say we were ***in*** darkness as we tend to read. Look again and realize it says we ***were*** darkness: "You were formerly darkness." God has changed us from darkness to light. We aren't just "in" the light now, we ***are*** light. This passage shows us our new nature is light. Salvation is evidently not about improving our nature. Read further:

"We were therefore buried with him through baptism into death in order that, just as Christ was raised from the dead through the glory of the Father, we, too, may live a new life···For we know that our old self was crucified with him so that the body of sin might be rendered powerless, that we should no longer be slaves to sin···Now if we died with Christ, we believe we will also live with him···In the same way, count yourselves dead to sin but alive to God in Christ Jesus" (Romans 6:4, 6, 8, 11).

This passage is clear that new life ***is*** ours. It is essential for us to understand: "Jesus doesn't offer to improve us. He offers to die and then to inhabit our personalities with His presence."[1] It was a one-time transformation. We became a new person in Christ, declared by God to be a saint when we said "yes" to Christ. We were justified ("just as if I'd never sinned"; Romans 3:24, 5:1, 8:30).

Therefore, since we have been justified through faith, we have peace with God through our Lord Jesus Christ.
Romans 5:1

We don't get 60% of Jesus in us upon salvation and then strive the rest of our days to get the other 40%. The full life of Christ dwells in us now.

The point is so frequently forgotten, but critical to negotiating our lives. If we view our salvation simply as a contractual agreement guaranteeing a happy eternity, we will struggle. Why? Where does that leave us in facing the difficulty of earthly life? If we are united with the One who overcame everything, yet still cannot sense His victory in our lives, perhaps it's because we haven't really believed that the exchange has occurred. If

The Spirit himself testifies with our spirit that we are God's children. Now if we are children, then we are heirs—heirs of God and co-heirs with Christ, if indeed we share in his sufferings in order that we may also share in his glory.
Romans 8:16-17

He saved us through the washing of rebirth and renewal by the Holy Spirit, whom he poured out on us generously through Jesus Christ our Savior, so that, having been justified by his grace, we might become heirs having the hope of eternal life.
Titus 3:5-7

Therefore, there is now no condemnation for those who are in Christ Jesus.
Romans 8:1

we view ourselves as people trying hard to improve, working to make bad habits good and sinful tendencies go away, we will fail. Paul is clear – Jesus took our sinful selves into the grave with Him and gave us a resurrected life instead.

Only when we view our salvation as a life exchange – "a once-profane existence now traded for a Holy Substitute" – this is when we begin to thrive, not survive.[2] Think about your life thus far. Would you say you have been surviving: getting by, just barely making it, watching the clock until it's time for bed? Or would you say you have been thriving: enjoying the people around you, breathing deep the rhythm of your life, contented in your soul? You, child of God, are a joint heir with Christ! You have the hope of life eternal! You have been released from condemnation! You are imbued with great purpose in the story of all ages! You are filled with peace and joy! You can conquer anything this world throws at you! You were meant to thrive!!

John 10:10 says it plainly:

"The thief comes only in order to steal and kill and destroy. I came that they may have and enjoy life, and have it in abundance (to the full, till it overflows)." (Amplified)

"A thief is only there to steal and kill and destroy. I came so they can have real and eternal life, more and better life than they ever dreamed of." (Message)

Are you living a "more and better life" than you ever dreamed of?!? If not, perhaps you have not understood the basis of your new life. Being born again transformed you into someone who didn't exist before. You were dead and then raised, now a spiritually born child of God, a child of light, a citizen of heaven. You didn't just get forgiveness, a Heaven ticket, and a new set of rules. No, your deepest identity now is that you died with Christ and your life is now hidden in Him.

This total reality of our life is what Jesus did for us on the Cross on the third day. That's why in Romans 6:11, Paul said, "Count yourselves dead to sin but alive to God in Christ Jesus." To "count" on something is to place all our hope in it; to believe it. We "count on" our friend to arrive around 2:00 when she said she would, water to flow when we turn it on, I-beams over our heads, and elastic in our pants. We don't think twice about those things, but move on as though they are infallibly true. The same mental mustering is the paradigm required by our faith. We Christians will only experience the joy and power and victory of life in Christ when we count on having been crucified with Him and raised in His life. We must know it, depend on it, function unquestionably upon its truth, cling to it as rock-solid as the day we graduated, birthed a child, lost a parent, or signed a contract.

Do you count on the fact that you are dead to sin but alive in Christ? Do you bank everything on the truth that you are meant to thrive in God's truest picture of you?

As you begin this study guide, be reminded of the words from Mufasa, the Lion King. He told his struggling son, "You are more than what you have become." You, too, are much more than the sum total of your days so far. With excitement, let us begin the process of uncovering and reclaiming the masterpiece for the credit and honor it was intended to give the Artist. The host of heaven is behind you, the power that raised Christ from the dead within you, and an incredible future ahead of you.

Reflect

What do you long for that you know you are not experiencing right now?

Do you believe God promised this for you as His child? Why or why not?

On page 13, Tammy writes, "Doesn't it feel like we're insatiable?" In what ways is this true for you?

Would you say you have been a person who falls into the category of someone looking to "get" or looking to give?

Why do you think this has characterized you?

What speaks to your soul from these verses?

For whoever wants to save his life will lose it, but whoever loses his life for me will save it. What good is it for a man to gain the whole world, and yet lose or forfeit his very self? Luke 9:24-25

Self-help is no help at all. Self-sacrifice is the way, my way, to finding yourself, your true self. What good would it do to get everything you want and lose you, the real you? Luke 9:24 (Message)

When you think about who you were as a young child, your personality, temperament, passions, and preferences, what do you think your intended self was to be? In other words, describe you without the damage... the real you.

All my longings lie open before you, O Lord; my sighing is not hidden from you.
Psalm 38:9

Through these he has given us his very great and precious promises, so that through them you may participate in the divine nature and escape the corruption in the world caused by evil desires.
2 Peter 1:4

Their destiny is destruction, their god is their stomach, and their glory is in their shame. Their mind is on earthly things.
Philippians 3:19

Write a prayer here expressing your heart to God about this whole matter of your hopes for healing and restoration:

Resolve

...without stain or wrinkle or any other blemish, but holy and blameless.
Ephesians 5:27

Those who look to him are radiant; their faces are never covered with shame.
Psalm 34:5

...what is man that you are mindful of him, the son of man that you care for him? You made him a little lower than the heavenly beings and crowned him with glory and honor.
Psalm 8:4-5

What truths do I feel God wanted me to receive in working through this chapter?

The Intended Plan
Chapter One

Refresh

Every masterpiece immediately makes us admire the creator of such beauty.

This chapter begins with two necessary elements to understand for true soul healing: God, and His idea of restoration. If we believe that we are God's workmanship, marred and grimed over by life's assaults, then restoration makes sense.

We are God's workmanship created in Christ Jesus to do good works, which God prepared in advance for us to do.
Ephesians 2:10

In other words, we can't proceed with healing until we believe the truth that we have been crucified and raised with Christ. Seen in this regard, restoration becomes about getting everything off and away from us that is covering the true masterwork underneath. We work through damage from hurts of all kinds, rubbing out spots, wiping away residue, mending torn areas of our hearts, so that Christ's life in us may be revealed. It's Jesus in plain sight, with us as the projection screen. What an awesome thing!!

However, too many Christians simply see themselves as sinners trying to be better Christians. In the process, they end up feeling inferior, insecure, inadequate, guilty, worried, or doubtful. Is that how you've been? Maybe you haven't realized that you don't get the abundant life by straining for it, reading about it, or immersing yourself in church activities. We *have* the abundant life. Not wish we have it, or on our way to it through greater effort, but it's ours now. When we gave our lives to Jesus, we got His in return.

Picture your hands and arms full with a box. Now imagine a larger, perfect box filled with everything you need and want. No one can put the better box in your arms until you do what? Put the other one down! It's an exchange. So, instead of striving for and praying for the resurrected life, our job is to accept it and live it.

Perhaps we struggle so much because we're reminded of our old nature often and we let it speak louder than God's promises to us. Instead, we must realize the Christian life – our abundant life in Jesus – is His and only He knows how to live it. Let yourself be convinced of this reality, trust deeply, think about it often, and obsess about how to give Jesus reign in your heart.

Christ is your life.
Colossians 3:4

Our job is to learn to walk in agreement with our new nature. Until we do that, we won't experience the abundant life of Christ. No one can consistently behave in a way different from how he or she perceives one's self. This is why many Christians are disenchanted with the Christian life. They aren't sensing the joy, peace, and purpose they want as a Christ follower. If we truly believe that we are God's specially designed and chosen children, we will eventually act like it. However, if we see ourselves as people trying really hard to be good, straining to squash sinful tendencies, and overcome bad habits, then God's promise of abundance will indeed seem a far cry from our daily reality.

For as he thinks in his heart, so is he.
Proverbs 23:7 (NKJV)

Our hope for healing, change, growth, and fulfillment as a Christian can only be based upon our understanding of who we are as children of God, completely indwelt by the Holy Spirit. You are a child of God – period.

How great is the love the Father has lavished on us, that we should be called children of God! And that is what we are!
1 John 3:1

You can't become any more of a child of God than what your spiritual birth gave you.[3] Our efforts of healing must begin by placing our efforts into believing that this is true, rather than trying harder to make it better.

We possess the fullness of His Spirit, but often do not live in that reality. Do you feel second-rate? You are a child of God seated with Christ in the heavenlies (Ephesians 2:6). Do you feel inadequate? You can do all things through Christ who strengthens you (Philippians 4:13). Alone? Your God will never leave you nor forsake you (Hebrews 13:5). Guilty? There is no condemnation for those who are in Christ (Romans 8:1). Confused? God provides wisdom for the asking (James 1:5). Worried? God gives peace and comfort in the place of our anxiety (Philippians 4:6, 1 Peter 5:7, John 14:27). When we don't live in the truths of God about His provision and our identity, it's as though we are limping on crutches even though our legs are completely healthy.

We have a choice today, right now. Galatians 5:1 says, "It is for freedom that Christ set you free." We can either believe we are free or not. When slavery ended and the plantations were unlocked, we imagine that all the slaves ran as fast as they could away from their masters, reveling in their freedom to be and do whatever they wanted. However, in actuality, many of the newly freed servants actually stayed, opting for known enslavement rather than newfound freedom. Many of us, by our unbelief, are doing the same, and wonder why our lives are so upside down. ***We aren't living according to our true identity!***

You will know the truth and the truth will set you free.
John 8:32

This chapter provides Scriptural basis for lifelong change and true healing. But we must have ***belief***. We must believe in the life we've been given.

Now the Lord is Spirit and where the Spirit of the Lord is, there is freedom.
2 Corinthians 3:17

Reflect - A Primer on God

What is God's idea of restoration?

He restores my soul.
Psalm 23:3

Restore us, O God; make your face shine upon us, that we may be saved.
Psalm 80:3

"So there is hope for your future," declares the Lord.
Jeremiah 31:17

Have you ever noticed that intense professional basketball games, filled with 48 minutes of massive talent and whizbang shotmaking, quite often come down to a simple foul shot? No matter how complex the level of play gets, it seems one can never stray too far from the basic essential of the game. That's why even superior athletes must practice vital free-throwing every day. It's because, in one sense, if you don't have the foul shot, the rest of the game won't matter.

We have a distinctly similar reality when it comes to "foul shots of faith." In other words, there are certain truths that we must go over and over, repetitiously, daily, or we won't make it through the day. Just as everything else in the complex game of basketball is built around the fundamentals, so is it with us and faith. If we do not build our perspectives, beliefs, and lives around indispensable truths, we will struggle significantly. Circumstances will cause us to careen, people's opinions will become obsessively important, and earthly endeavors will seem purposeless unless we begin and end with the "foul shots of faith."

The basic elements of every minute of our lives, the building blocks for everything we know and believe, must be completely enveloped in these truths which comprise the foul shots of faith:

Foul Shot #1:

God is unconditionally ______________________________.

And I pray that you, being rooted and established in love, may have power, together with all the saints, to grasp how wide and long and high and deep is the love of Christ. Ephesians 3:17-18

How great is the love the Father has lavished on us, that we should be called children of God! And that is what we are! The reason the world does not know us is that it did not know him. 1 John 3:1

...neither height nor depth, nor anything else in all creation, will be able to separate us from the love of God that is in Christ Jesus our Lord. Romans 8:39

Give thanks to the Lord, for he is good; his love endures forever. Psalm 118:1

The Lord appeared to us in the past, saying: "I have loved you with an everlasting love; I have drawn you with loving-kindness." Jeremiah 31:3

Whoever does not love does not know God, because God is love. 1 John 4:8

When it comes to God's amazing, unique, relentless, passionate, constant, all-encompassing, lavish love for you, which of the two reactions described on page 19 do you tend to have? Are you apt to breeze over it or more likely to believe it's not true for you?

Why do you think this is so?

When you hear the word "Father," what adjectives come to mind?

How do you feel when you realize God loves you with a love that is one-way, completely sacrificial, much like a little baby held in its parents' arms? This infant does nothing but take, try, and inconvenience the parents, and yet their love is enormous, effusive, and seemingly boundless. Have you ever considered that you are God's baby?

Foul Shot #2:

God is always ______________________________.

Never will I leave you; never will I forsake you. Hebrews 13:5

Where can I go from you Spirit? Where can I flee from you presence? If I go up to the heavens, you are there; if I make my bed in the depths, you are there. If I rise on the wings of the dawn, if I settle on the far side of the sea, even there your hand will guide me, you right hand will hold me fast. Psalm 139:7-10

For great is his love toward us, and the faithfulness of the Lord endures forever. Praise the Lord. Psalm 117:2

And my God will meet all your needs according to his glorious riches in Christ Jesus. Philippians 4:19

Now to the King eternal, immortal, invisible, the only God, be honor and glory for ever and ever. Amen. 1 Timothy 1:17

God's presence is constantly with his children. How does the concept of having God "smack dab glued to your side" bring comfort to you?

How does this concept disturb you?

Describe a time you have been aware of God's presence recently.

What affect did knowing that have on you?

Can you envision Him with you even now, this minute? What visual do you have of His presence? How does this help make real for you that He is Emmanuel, God ***with*** us, in your life?

What could you do this week to further your awareness of God's loving presence?

> "Often, in the midst of great problems, we stop short of the real blessing God has for us, which is a fresh vision of who he is.
>
> Anne Graham Lotz"

Foul Shot #3:

God gives complete ______________________________.

When you were dead in your sins and in the uncircumcision of your sinful nature, God made you alive with Christ. He forgave us all our sins. Colossians 2:13

But God demonstrates his own love for us in this: While we were still sinners, Christ died for us. Romans 5:8

Praise the Lord, O my soul, and forget not all his benefits-who forgives all your sins and heals all your diseases…. Psalm 103:2-3

“ There is nothing, absolutely nothing, that God will not forgive. You cannot "out-sin" His forgiveness. You cannot "out-sin" the love of God.

Kathy Troccoli 

What are some areas of my life that I try to hide from God?

Tammy points out on page 22 that a primary reason Christians don't experience a deep and fruitful relationship with Christ is that they do not grasp the significance of their forgiveness. To develop a deeper understanding of forgiveness, meditate on these verses on forgiveness. Which one do you believe would be beneficial to memorize?

Acts 13:38
Micah 7:18
Eph 1:7
Col 1:13-14
Col 3:13
1 John 1:9
1 John 2:12
Romans 8:1
Isaiah 1:18
2 Corinthians 5:17

Write it out here:

If we have great difficulty forgiving ourselves for something, even when we accept God's enormous gift of full and complete absolution of our every sin, this is a serious problem. To choose to hold onto something God has released is basically telling God we have higher standards than He provided through the mutilation and suffocation of His sinless son. Perhaps you didn't realize that not forgiving yourself for something was doing this. Let today be the day you are once and for all free from your sin, not only before God, but also in your own eyes, from your sin. Praise His name!

Because of Jesus' tremendous sacrifice, I now choose by faith to believe God has forgiven me for...

Or, as a reminder to your own soul, thank Jesus for what you know He has forgiven you for...

Foul Shot #4:

God is full of ______________________ and _________________________.

For it is by grace you have been saved, through faith—and this not from yourselves, it is the gift of God. Ephesians 2:8

Come near to God and he will come near to you. Wash your hands, you sinners, and purify your hearts, you double-minded. James 4:8

And he passed in front of Moses, proclaiming, "The Lord, the Lord, the compassionate and gracious God, slow to anger, abounding in love and faithfulness." Exodus 34:6

The Lord is gracious and compassionate, slow to anger and rich in love. Psalm 145:8

The Word became flesh and made his dwelling among us. We have seen his glory, the glory of the One and Only, who came from the Father, full of grace and truth. John 1:14

Yet the Lord longs to be gracious to you; he rises to show you compassion. For the Lord is a God of justice. Blessed are all who wait for him! Isaiah 30:18

Reflect on these definitions of "grace":

- unmerited divine assistance given humans for their regeneration or sanctification
- virtue coming from God
- approval, favor
- special favor, privilege
- when you get what you don't deserve

and of "mercy":

- compassion or forbearance shown especially to an offender or to one subject to another's power
- compassionate treatment
- a blessing that is an act of divine favor or compassion
- when you don't get the punishment you do deserve

When considered in light of these definitions, Isaiah 30:18 is overwhelming, perhaps even shocking, in its reminder of God's character. It affirms,

"Yet the Lord longs to be gracious to you; he rises to show you compassion."

When we long for something, we can't wait for it. Think of craving that special meal, counting the minutes until we meet up with our friend, on pins and needles until our package arrives in the mail, desperately yearning for when our kids come home on Christmas break, aching for a needed hug or so excited for vacation you can't sleep the night before. Unbelievably, this is God's desire for us – He can't wait to show us special favor. It's like He is leaning forward on the edge of His seat to show us approval, give us a gift, and give us free help.

Then, "he rises to show you compassion" give us the sense that he woke up this morning for the purpose of showing us tenderness, kindness, and forgiveness. In human language, it's as though giving us compassion instead of condemnation was the first thing on His mind.

The posture depicted in this verse is so astounding that we often can't grasp it. We wait for punishment; He gives presents. We hold our breath for the reminder of our failure, He hands us a blessed new future.

To bring home this point, God gave us the picture of the prodigal's father in Luke 15:11-32.

Not only was the son sinning horribly by squandering all of his father's good fortune and blessing, he was doing so intentionally. Yet, when we read of this father's attitude towards his wayward son, we do not see anger, punishment, shame, or even frustration. Instead, we behold the polar opposite – this father is straining his eyes, scanning the horizon, looking for the first sign of the son's return. Upon that return, the father is so anxious to bless the son, he runs to him and envelops him in a huge bear hug

But while he was still a long way off, his father saw him and was filled with compassion for him; he ran to his son, threw his arms around him and kissed him.
Luke 15:20

He was clearly a father longing to be gracious, rising to show compassion to his child.

How does this picture of God change or reaffirm your perspective of His grace and mercy?

Another striking picture of these non-negotiable truths about God is found in Lamentations 3:22-23. It says,

"Because of the Lord's great love we are not consumed, for his compassions never fail. They are new every morning; great is your faithfulness."

We see all four "foul shots" here – His love, His faithfulness, His forgiveness, and His mercy. Many versions actually translate this passage using the word "mercy," such as:

"The faithful love of the Lord never ends! His mercies never cease. Great is his faithfulness; his mercies begin afresh each morning." (NLT)

Once again, we are given a pictorial truth about the character of our God with massive implications for everyday living. His love is so unconditional, His faithfulness so vast, and His forgiveness so complete, we have a "reset" button anytime, anywhere, for anything in our lives! It's true, because of Christ, the chalkboard that lists our failings, short comings, and sins is erased. Each moment is a true new beginning in Jesus when we turn to our God. This is why, no matter what has happened, no matter what you have done, no matter what others have done to you, ***"we are not consumed"***. What glorious words for we who sin regularly and have much in our lives and hearts that seeks to consume us! His mercy is new every moment, because He alone is 100% faithful to His promises.

But I, when I am lifted up from the earth, will draw all men to myself.
John 12:32

Referring back to the definitions of "mercy," record your understanding of Lamentations 3:22-23:

Luke 13:34 says that God longs to gather His children to Himself. He is orchestrating a winning, wooing process in our lives for us to be drawn to Him alone.

How have you seen God woo you in your life?

Just like basketball players must practice free throws over and over daily in order for them to become the most natural motion they possess on the court, we, too must wake up daily and have these foul shots of faith in our consciousness. Think of how much different each day would go for you if you held these truths right in front of your face every minute – that you are loved without regard for your performance, totally forgiven, wrapped up in the faithfulness of a God who won't ever let you go, and given undeserved gifts and privileges. It's not hard to see how our daily interactions are radically different when we build the rest of life upon this foundation.

Which one of the four foul shots of faith is the most challenging for you to hold onto?

1. God is unconditionally loving.
2. God is always faithful.
3. God gives complete forgiveness.
4. God is full of grace and mercy.

Reflect - A Primer on Us

Holding onto such life-altering truth with fervor is enough to bring healing to our lives. However, we are also brought deeper into God's restorative process when we rest our identity solely on God. So often, we look for our definition of who we are in other people, in circumstances, in possessions, and in performance, wondering why we feel so out of sorts so often.

If you recall reading the children's book *Are You My Mother?*, you remember that the little birdie is roving around, desperately asking everyone and everything if it is his mother. From a cow to a crane in a junkyard, the poor tiny thing is never at rest until it finally encounters the one who birthed him. It's the same with us. Until we rest our identity squarely on what the One who created us says we are, we will simply be on a fruitless search, constantly discomfited by our lack of security.

On pages 24 and following, we read that we have positional power. As believers, we have a whole host of gifts, blessings, and privileges that are ours only because Jesus Christ purchased us with His blood, and we are the children of God. In the *Band of Brothers*, one scene depicts an officer reminding another, "We salute the rank, not the man." The same is true of us. We are branded as "Christ's" and so are given power from that position alone, not dependent upon our own merit.

In similar fashion, have you ever noticed how the children of famous artists and performers are given privileged access and leeway simply because of who their parents are, regardless of the actual work ethic, talent, or capability of that child? They are given a level of influence, honor, and privilege only because of the family into which they were born. Even more so is that analogy true for us as chosen children of the Most High.

Describe your deepening realization of what positional power is:

As we view ourselves through the lens of positional power, just like the foul shots of faith, we must stand securely on God's thoughts of who we are. We must do this especially in the face of a world wanting to assault our identity. Which of these truths about you below is the hardest for you to embrace? Circle it.

My true identity is a child of God and He lavishes me with love. 1 John 3:1

He loves and delights in me. Jeremiah 31:3

I am completely forgiven. Colossians 2:13

He longs to show me grace and compassion. Isaiah 30:18

I have a specific and unique purpose to do good things for Him. Ephesians 2:10

I am a bright light no matter where I go. Matthew 5:14

I am being changed to be more like Jesus. Philippians 1:6

Perhaps reviewing characteristics about yourself as a child of God will help. For each descriptor below of who you are in Jesus, jot a verse you find about it, thank God for the truth of it, or simply try to allow it to sink in.

Powerful:

Purposeful:

Delightful:

Impactful:

Special:

Chosen:

Our feelings, though wonderful gifts from the Lord, often betray us in this area. Some days we will feel great, some days not so great. Whatever the day, whatever the feeling, the truth of God about who we are remains true no matter what.

Write a prayer here about choosing His truth about you over your own feelings about yourself:

To aid you in cementing God's perspective of you in your heart and mind, here are more Scriptures about who you are because of Jesus[4]:

I am accepted in Christ

John 1:12	I am God's child
John 15:15	I am Christ's friend
Romans 5:1	I have been justified
1 Corinthians 6:17	I am united with the Lord and one with Him in spirit
1 Corinthians 6:20	I have been bought with a price; I belong to God
1 Corinthians 12:27	I am a member of Christ's body
Ephesians 1:1	I am a saint
Ephesians 1:5	I have been adopted as God's child
Ephesians 2:18	I have direct access to God through the Holy Spirit
Colossians 1:14	I have been redeemed and forgiven of all my sins
Colossians 2:10	I am complete in Christ

I am secure in Christ

Romans 8:1,2	I am free forever from condemnation
Romans 8:28	I am assured that all things work together for good
Romans 8:33, 34	I am free from any condemning charges against me
Romans 8:35	I cannot be separated from the love of God
2 Corinthians 1:21	I have been established, anointed, and sealed by God
Colossians 3:3	I am hidden with Christ in God
Philippians 1:6	I am confident that the good work God has begun in me will be perfected
Philippians 3:20	I am a citizen of heaven
2 Timothy 1:7	I have not been given a spirit of fear, but of power, love and a sound mind
Hebrews 4:16	I can find grace and mercy in time of need
1 John 5:18	I am born of God and the evil one cannot touch me

I am significant in Christ

Matthew 5:13,14	I am the salt and light of the earth
John 15:15	I am branch of the true vine, a channel of His life
John 15:16	I have been chosen and appointed to bear fruit
Acts 1:8	I am a personal witness of Christ's
1 Corinthians 3:16	I am God's temple
2 Cor. 5:17-20	I am a minister of reconciliation
2 Corinthians 6:1	I am God's coworker
Ephesians 2:6	I am seated with Christ in the heavenly realm
Ephesians 2:10	I am God's workmanship
Ephesians 3:12	I may approach God with freedom and confidence
Philippians 4:13	I can do all things through Christ who strengthens me

Look up some of the Scriptures listed and choose some of them to rewrite in your own words. You might try personalizing them, adding your own name.

Rachel, because you are in Christ, you are free from condemnation so you don't have to feel guilty that your house is not as spotless as your neighbor's always seems to be.

Now, without looking above for "answers," try seeing how firmly you are believing God's truth about you.

Because I am His,

I am ___________________________

I am ___________________________

I am ___________________________

I am ___________________________

Thank you, Jesus, that because of you alone, I am ___________________________!

How am I going to hang on to these truths God has shown me?

How is your life different (or how would it be different) when you are mindful of the truth that God has created you for good works?

His divine power has given us everything we need for life and godliness through our knowledge of him who called us by his own glory and goodness. 2 Peter 1:3

Record your reaction to this truth.

Resolve

The intent of this chapter has been to provide an immovable, massive basis of security in God's truth. The reason for such a thrust at the beginning of a book on healing is that no true cure can occur without a solid foundation. We could attempt to wipe away the grime and dirt from a painting, but unless we were certain it was a priceless masterpiece made by an extraordinary creator, we wouldn't be as committed and confident as necessary in our reclamation project.

The certainty of our foundation is critical. When we know who God is and who we are through His Son, we can build our lives, our souls, our healing upon those truths. In this way, Jesus is very practically the cornerstone to which Scripture refers. "See, I lay a stone in Zion, a chosen and precious cornerstone, and the one who trusts in him will never be put to shame" (1 Peter 2:6). "Cornerstone" refers to the first stone set in the construction of masonry, where all other stones are set in reference to this one, determining the position of the entire structure. It's called the "foundation stone" and provides an indispensable and fundamental basis for everything else.

Such is the truth covered in this chapter. Jesus, and all truth about God we discover in the Word and through the Spirit, is the first, middle, and last of everything we need. If our chief aim is not Jesus, we will not be content. If our chief pursuit is not Christ, we will not be satiated. If our foundation is not Jesus, the rest of our lives will not line up. The truths of Christ – our cornerstone (Ephesians 2:20) – provide the kind of strength and security we need to build our hopes for deep and lasting change... forever.

So if the Son sets you free, you will be free indeed. John 8:36

Consequently, you are no longer foreigners and aliens, but fellow citizens with God's people and members of God's household, built on the foundation of the apostles and prophets, with Christ Jesus himself as the chief cornerstone.
Ephesians 2:19-20

Full Awareness
Chapter Two

Do not be afraid or discouraged because of this vast army. For the battle is not yours, but God's.
2 Chronicles 20:15

You armed me with strength for battle; you made my adversaries bow at my feet.
Psalm 18:39

Put on the full armor of God so that you can take your stand against the devil's schemes.
Ephesians 6:11

Be on your guard; stand firm in the faith; be men of courage; be strong.
1 Corinthians 16:13

Fight the good fight of the faith.
1 Timothy 6:12

Refresh

If you've ever seen the Indiana Jones or National Treasure movies, you know the plot revolves around reclaiming a rare, hidden treasure. The combatants must face multiple enemies, potential death, and myriad battles before garnering the prized possession. There are thrills; there are times of desperation. There are defeats along the way, and great perseverance is required. However, the beauty and value of the recovered riches, along with the character transformation undergone by the seekers making the journey, is well worth the fight.

This is your story as well, masterpiece of God. Your intended self – God's best design for you and your part in His revealing His Son – is the covered-up gem. There is a massive assault raging against your efforts to possess such treasure by living in the truths of God. At every turn, there is another assailant and another battle. The sheer worth of the prize is validated by the level of opposition encountered in retrieving it. There is a fight raging over you, even now, because of your value to the God who made you, loves you, and purchased your victory with His own blood.

This chapter begins with sections called, "The Larger Canvas" and "Seeing the Right Battle." It would be helpful to stop and assess, "What is the larger canvas and the right battle?" In fact, asking ourselves this question throughout the day, every day, would be life-changing. It's as though we are players on a stage, who need to be aware of the scenery dropped in behind them. What is the backdrop of your days?

Simply put, Christians are soldiers in an army at war. Scripture is soaked with references to fighting, allusions to war, and indications of enemies.

We are commanded to engage in militant actions such as resisting, fighting, and wearing armor.

This battle, though, is one not against flesh and blood, but one waged in the spiritual realm.

For our struggle is not against flesh and blood, but against the rulers, against the authorities, against the powers of this dark world and against the spiritual forces of evil in the heavenly realms. Ephesians 6:12

Other versions translate the battle as "fighting" or "wrestling." Whatever the picture, the Bible starkly indicates that the spiritual battle is more real than anything we can take in with our five senses. We aren't fighting "flesh and blood," but spiritual forces of evil.

Put succinctly:

- There is a spiritual war going on between good and evil, between God's kingdom and satan's kingdom.
- All believers are involved in this war and it rages all around us, whether we are aware of it or not.
- Most people are not aware of the spiritual war as they go through their everyday life.

In a very true sense, the presence of an unseen enemy stalking you closely is more of a reality than the chair you sit on right now. That's why we are told to "fix our eyes not on what is seen, but on what is unseen. For what is seen is temporary, but what is unseen is eternal" (2 Corinthians 4:18). Only when we come to grips with the fact that we are actually in a spiritual war zone every day of our lives - no matter how organized or calm things may seem to the outside viewer - will we truly start to taste deep and abiding victory. If not, we will misinterpret most of what is happening around us and to us.

In this chapter, Tammy explains this spiritual battle development:

1. When we live and love freely in God's strength, His plan, and through His Son, God is glorified. (People admire the creator when they behold a masterpiece.)

2. Because of this, the enemy wants to take you out – steal, kill, and destroy. There is no end to the relentless assault, specifically designed and targeted for us.

3. The plan tailored for our destruction includes the ways in which we have been wounded on this earth, which cause us to be relationally tentative, isolated, or self-protective.

4. Every person has been wounded, and tends to fall in the category of paying too much or too little attention to the damage from life's hurts.

5. Because of God's amazing grace and mercy, absolutely every wound we've had in life, whether terrible or tiny, can be turned around and used for our good and to bring God even greater glory.

6. For that to happen, we cannot fall prey to hell's number one weaponry – lies.

7. Deceit, lies, and accusation are the main ways that hellish minions attempt to steal, kill, and destroy our faith in God, love for others, and truths about ourselves.

8. Recognizing this larger canvas and fighting the right battle allows the child of God to move out of the past and into God's plan for full restoration.

Reflect

As you reflect on the following questions, remember that evil hates us because we uniquely reveal the glory of God. Because it can't destroy God, evil will seek to do awful damage to human beings who, in bearing His very image, display the glory of the Almighty. Evil works to destroy that glory by stealing and marring what makes us most glorious – our capacity to live and love through the power of Christ within us. We can't heal unless we clearly see how evil works to wreck us.

If evil is ultimately after the glory of God, why is evil after me/bent on my destruction?

A verse that captures the entire picture of this chapter, wherein Jesus aptly sums up the war we are in, is John 10:9, 10:

"I am the gate; whoever enters through me will be saved. He will come in and go out, and find pasture. The thief comes only to steal and kill and destroy; I have come that they may have life, and have it to the full."

Jesus warned that a thief would be trying to take us out, so why are we so surprised when it seems like an enemy is trying to destroy us? Seen from this vantage point, all of life is spiritual warfare since satan is trying to destroy us.

How do you think hell has tried to steal from you, kill you, or destroy you? Be specific.

When my dad left without telling me first, I was devastated and have had a hard time trusting anybody since.

As you recall, the power that raised Christ from the dead now resides fully in you. What is your reaction to seeing the things you wrote listed above in black and white?

Similarly, which of these things that has happened to you that was meant for evil can you pray that God will turn around and use for good?

You intended to harm me, but God intended it for good to accomplish what is now being done, the saving of many lives.
Genesis 50:20

Write that prayer here:

How have you already seen Him take something meant for evil and turn it around and use it for good?

What was meant for evil	God's resulting good
My family had no money growing up. Evil wanted me to see myself as white trash.	*My good friends and even some of my neighbors ask for my help in finding good deals.*

Review a few Scriptural examples of this divine turn-around:

Genesis 45:1-15, 50:16-21 *Joseph's brothers really did him wrong...*

John 9:1-12

2 Corinthians 12:7-10

While it can be unnerving to realize that satan has schemes against us, to identify comforting aspects of these truths will help you overcome both naiveté and fear.

Scriptural Truth	How this helps me in my battling
1 Peter 5:6-9	
James 4:7	
Ephesians 6:10-17	
2 Corinthians 2:11	

When Ephesians 6:12 reminds me that my battle is not against flesh and blood ("For our struggle is not against flesh and blood, but against the rulers, against the authorities, against the powers of this dark world and against the spiritual forces of evil in the heavenly realms."), this means my struggle isn't against:

____

(put the names of "flesh and blood" here, like "John," "my boss," even "myself," etc.).

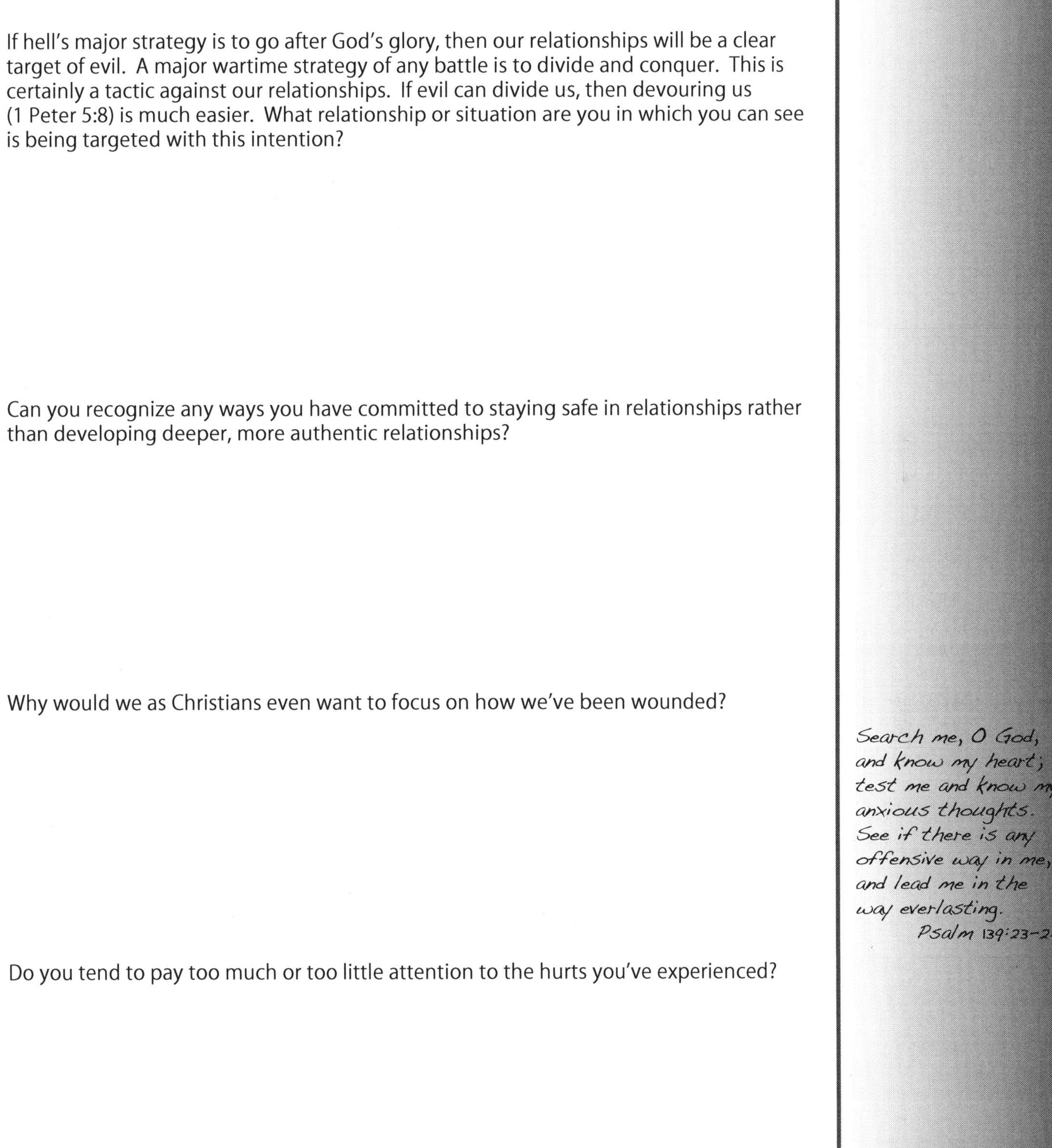

If hell's major strategy is to go after God's glory, then our relationships will be a clear target of evil. A major wartime strategy of any battle is to divide and conquer. This is certainly a tactic against our relationships. If evil can divide us, then devouring us (1 Peter 5:8) is much easier. What relationship or situation are you in which you can see is being targeted with this intention?

Can you recognize any ways you have committed to staying safe in relationships rather than developing deeper, more authentic relationships?

Why would we as Christians even want to focus on how we've been wounded?

*Search me, O God,
and know my heart;
test me and know my
anxious thoughts.
See if there is any
offensive way in me,
and lead me in the
way everlasting.
Psalm 139:23-24*

Do you tend to pay too much or too little attention to the hurts you've experienced?

Describe how you understand that evil can gain a foothold through pain from your past.

Why is this so dangerous?

Tammy explains on pages 42-43 that our pain can become an idol if left unexamined. What does this mean?

He was a murderer from the beginning, not holding to the truth, for there is no truth in him. When he lies, he speaks his native language, for he is a liar and the father of lies.
John 8:44b

The war we are in is an all-out assault on the truth of the exchange of Christ's life for yours, as we covered in the past two chapters. Think of it as a constant pelting and pummeling of all truth about who God is and who we are. To lie relentlessly to us about God, ourselves, and others is satan's major plan. We saw his very first attack against the human race was to lie to Adam and Eve about God and His plan. He is called the father of lies in John 8:44, where it says he is a murderer with no truth in him. It also says lying is his native language.

So, if one who speaks "lie" is masterminding the schemes to harm us, what will be the natural artillery used against us? Lies, confusion, deceit, accusation.

Therefore, any idea or impression that brings discouragement, condemnation, or confusion is not from God. How this works is that the enemy will try to play the ventriloquist, "throwing" its voice to sound like someone from your past, or your workplace, or even your own voice. Remember, this is a war in the *spirit* realm, so lies will come in the place of your spirit, in your soul. Even scholars in the secular realm acknowledge that there is a process by which the voice of others becomes our own

("You're stupid," "You'll never grow up," "Why can't you just be like your sister?"). Perhaps when described this way, we can see how evil is a master at subtly suggesting some untruth, hoping we'll buy into it.

In Revelation 12:10 and Zechariah 3:1, satan is called the "accuser" who is throwing accusatory assaults at the Lord's chosen ones.

In fact, it says we are accused day and night. It is critical to remember that satan is working overtime, continuously and persistently flooding our ears, eyes, and minds with ideas and suggestions meant to steal our faith, hope, and love. It is plain to see why the cornerstone of truth and the foul shots of faith are so critical as our foundation, given that it is being assailed every day, all day long.

For the accuser of our brothers, who accuses them before our God day and night, has been hurled down.
Revelation 12:10

The good news is that anytime we sense accusation, we know it is from hell itself. In this way, it's easy to catch on when evil is afoot. Like dashboard indicator lights on a car, when they go off, they tell us something is amiss with the vehicle. In kind, whenever you are overwhelmed with feelings of condemnation, thoughts of self-harm, massive confusion, significant doubt, waning faith, insinuations of purposelessness, lack of desire to move towards God, blanketing insecurity, besetting feelings of shame – anytime you experience these it is just like the dashboard lights telling you something is wrong. Accusation is occurring!

Do you know what accusation sounds like against yourself?

Submit yourselves, then, to God. Resist the devil, and he will flee from you.
James 4:7

It's important to remember that accusation is different from godly conviction. The result of accusation is always a decrease in faith, love, hope, or security in God's Word. Accusatory statements are things like: "Didn't you ask forgiveness for that last night, too? What makes you think God will forgive that again? Aren't you a supposed leader at church? You'll never fit in, because if they knew what you were really like, no one would want you there. What makes you think you have anything to offer? Even your own spouse seems dissatisfied with you. And to think you are some special vessel of Christ. What a joke." And on and on...

What accusations do you "hear"/feel on a regular basis? (There's no right or wrong answer here. Anything you can think of at all is good work. Being as specific as possible is very helpful too.) Name some of those accusations you find yourself struggling with often:

Be self controlled and alert. Your enemy the devil prowls around like a roaring lion looking for someone to devour.
1 Peter 5:8

While much of the rest of this study guide will help bring this to bear, it is great news to remember that we have no reason at all to fear! The fullness of Christ Jesus and His power reside in us now by His Spirit. So, evil has no power over us except what we give by being deceived into believing lies. Because hell's minions lost you eternally when you became a child of God, they can only try to neutralize your effectiveness for God now by trying to confuse your belief system, muddy your mind, weaken your faith, and wreck your emotions.

What are some lies evil regularly tries to tell me about:

God	Myself	Others
God will never forgive me for this.	*I'll always be this way It'll never get better.*	*God doesn't love me like He loves others. My husband wishes he had never married me.*

I have told you these things, so that in me you may have peace. In this world you will have trouble. But take heart! I have overcome the world.
John 16:33

Here's the good news about spending so much time on a "bad" subject (thinking about lies, deception, and accusation) – Scripture tells us it's so "that satan might not outwit us. For we are not unaware of his schemes" (2 Corinthians 2:11). Awareness – the knowledge of what is actually happening – is often in and of itself enough to bring about massive life-change. So, we are starting with awareness, following the Biblical admonition to expose evil's schemes against us. While we are uncovering and exposing hell's particular strategies against us here, we are going to clearly learn how to walk in victory and defeat these lies in chapters eight and nine.

What is one way you may be bowing down to your past, according to the description on pages 46-47?

What is a turn-it-around, shove-it-in-satan's-face prayer for restoration you have about your past?

> “ Every misfortune, every failure, every loss may be transformed. God has the power to transform all misfortunes into "God-sends."
>
> Mrs. Charles E. Cowman 

On page 49, Tammy says, "I pray we will have eyes and boldness to see what hurt we have, how evils wants to destroy us, that God has a plan to give us abundant life, how our lives are meant for God's glory and what accusation is being hurled against us this very moment." What is your response to this after having interacted with the truths in this chapter?

Expose some accusatory garbage that evil is trying to get you to listen to right now (about these truths, about yourself, about God's plan for you and your healing).

This spiritual battle stuff is over-the-top and doesn't apply to me.
You will never be able to fight this battle and feel like you are winning.

Now, take a big black marker and cross them out, with vigor and conviction!! (Or better yet, a red one to represent the blood of Christ!!)

Resolve

It is critical that Christians remember always that they are members of the army of God. For those who are reacting to the concept of war, this can be a struggle in itself. But when we refuse to see ourselves as soldiers, we limit the power of God in our lives and are weakened by the continual barrage of attacks that the enemy has planned and executed against the unarmed.

Incredibly, with the death and resurrection of Jesus Christ and the sending of the Holy Spirit, the Kingdom of God has now come to this earth and is located within the believer. Full resurrection victory resides in you!!! Therefore, when you engage the spiritual battle that exists, you will very soon be experiencing sustained victory, as well as inner peace and confidence in who you are.[5] This is all because:

"You, dear children, are from God and have overcome them, because the one who is in you is greater than the one who is in the world." (1 John 4:4)

Hallelujah and yippee!!

What truths do I feel God wanted me to receive in
working through this chapter?

Wounds, Lies, and Consequences
Chapter Three

He was despised and rejected by men, a man of sorrows, and familiar with suffering...Surely he took up our infirmities and carried our sorrows.
Isaiah 53:3a, 4a

Refresh

Don't you wonder how major lottery ticket winners handle that one small strip of paper until it is in the hands of those who redeem its worth? Do you put it in a safe, sleep with it, or pin it to your underwear? While this might be a stretch, the recovery of God's masterpiece in you relates to this lottery ticket. Your value to your rightful owner is massive – a greater fortune than any amount of money. Yet, God gave you to others to handle until the day when you are directly in His grasp again.

And just like if someone were to hand over the Mona Lisa to a 5-year-old, it's going to get damaged in the process, only because that immature owner doesn't realize what he has his hands on.

Much of what we need healing from is how evil has utilized the hurts, offenses, disappointments, and betrayals we have suffered at the hands of others. Many of the origins of our behavior and thinking today are found in past relational interactions, especially developmental ones. Our present emotional trouble is often a symptom of needs unmet or wounds committed either willingly or unintentionally at the hands of another. These hurts of the past can result in knee-jerk reactions today that don't honor God.

Restoration is not the resolution of our past. The goal is not to make sense of it all. Many things about our lives will never "make sense." So, if we look to the past with that hope, we will never experience healing. However, it is imperative for us to identify as many puzzle pieces as possible as to why we do not live in the full victory of Christ. Some pieces require comprehending past events, people, and contexts in order to draw us into deeper relationship with God and His purposes for our lives. This is the aim of our present chapter.

[Those who grieve in Zion] will rebuild the ancient ruins and restore the paces long devastated; they will renew the ruined cities that have been devastated for generations.
Isaiah 61:4

We will at best only find temporary relief unless we can uncover where and how evil found inroads to accuse us and lie to our souls. The primary fodder from which all hell wants to thwart God's plan for us is by using our past wounds against us. They provide hotbeds for accusation. Today, whenever we have a situation or person or event similar to a hurtful one in the past, it is a setup for evil to lie to us. Any enemy searches for the weakened opening. Many of our automatic emotional responses from our past have great bearing on what behaviors we engage in today, providing just such an opening.

The bottom line is that we need God's gracious insight to understand why we are the way we are and why we do much of what we do. From there, we need God's mighty strength to change. The questions following lay the groundwork for an understanding of your wounds that acknowledges the damage to your spirit while charting a path toward the abundant life God promises.[6]

Moving towards God's full life for us is the one and only reason for delving into our past. We want to expose the schemes of evil in our lives, unveil reasons behind our present behaviors and feelings, unlock secrets of our hearts, and live in the light of the Lord's great love and power. Our objective in sorting through and assessing past damage is for God's wisdom, that we may be fully His. We do this because,

"Surely you desire truth in the inner parts; you teach me wisdom in the inmost place." Psalm 51:6

It takes a hard look to have truth deep within. Many choose not to journey there. But our God urges:

"Wisdom is supreme; therefore get wisdom. Though it cost all you have, get understanding." Proverbs 4:7

"...get wisdom, discipline and understanding." Proverbs 23:23

May this section of reclaiming the museum-quality, awe-inspiring masterpiece of God that your soul is, provide you great wisdom to live out the rest of your days in truth and beauty.

Reflect

What is a wound of commission? Give some personal examples of this type of wound.

What is a wound of omission? Give some personal examples of this type of wound.

When we merge the concept of wounds together with the larger spiritual battle covered in the last chapter, we can easily see hell's plan is to implant as many lies as possible during times of hurt. Therefore, more often than not, our present emotional struggles are the symptom of a deeper wound where lies were originally implanted.

Identify two or three of the most significant wounds of your life thus far.
What lies could have taken root from them?

Wound	Lie that took root
In fifth grade Jan said she'd be my partner but picked someone else instead	*I'm not good enough* *I'm not important*

Describe how children's need for unconditional love looks in these stages:

Ages 0 – 5:

Think about cribs, diapers, learning to walk and talk, life's firsts, kindergarten, skinned knees...

Ages 6 – 11:

Think about action figures, baby dolls, Disney channel pop stars, American Idol, first forays into sports...

Ages 12 – 18:

Think about peer pressure, hormones, college decisions, growing responsibility, social anxiety, extracurricular pursuits, dating...

Ages 19 – on:

Think about transitioning into adulthood, no summer vacation, bills, job searches, posturing for the future, relationships, aging, seasons of life...

Read the descriptions of the people in Tammy's examples on pages 69-76. Is there one with which you especially identify? How?

Try to depict your own internal diagram for your vats. Like the example in the diagram on page 65, on the eight vats below, shade in the portion of unconditional love you feel you probably received during each stage of your life. Of these eight, circle your emptiest vat.

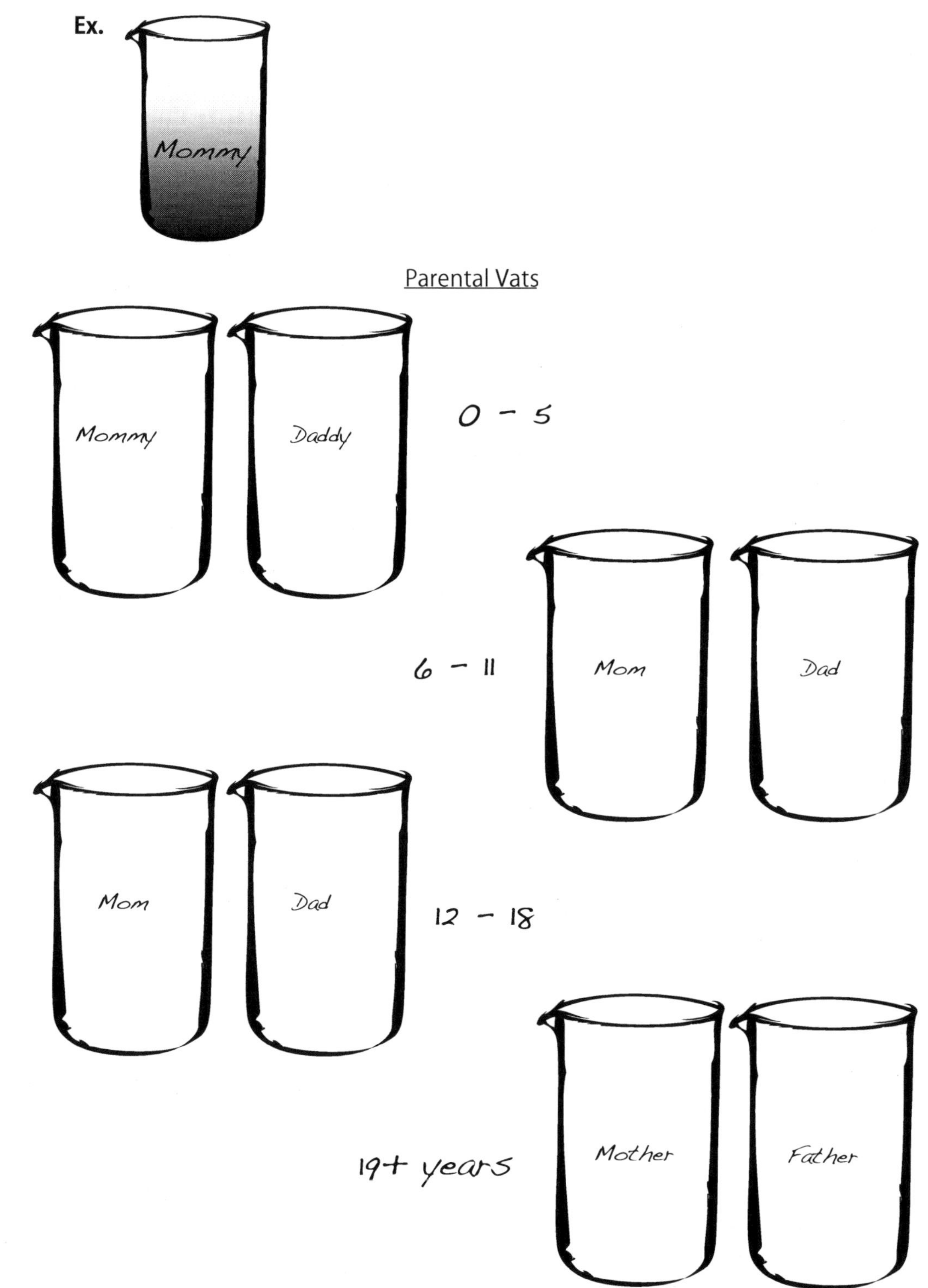

Skip these vats for now and go on to the next page

Other Vats

(friend, pastor, grandparent, mentor, etc.)

What can you see about yourself as you identify your emptiest parental "vat" and consider the idea that "our emptiest vat drives much of our present-day interactions?

Healing has to include awareness that we often relate to others on what we didn't get before. Because we live this side of heaven, not one person has every vat full. That's an important realization, because all too often, we live with constant disappointment because somewhere inside us, we think it is possible to have every vat full, and we've just been robbed. Moving beyond this perspective is critical to true soul restoration.

Return to the vat diagram on the previous page and label the vats for other significant relationships in your life (spouse vat, best friend vat, sibling vats, etc).

Shade in each vat to indicate the level of unconditional love you receive from the person for whom you labeled each vat.

As you sit back and analyze this representation of your internal reservoirs of love, can you identify a certain type of person to whom you are drawn that you can trace to an early deficit?

It's even possible you find yourself repelled by that same type of person, because you resent the fact that you "couldn't have that" or such a person is completely foreign to you. (An example would be the female who draws back from nurturing women because her own mother was so harsh.) Reflect here:

Now, draw arrows from the vats on the right to the vats on the left, showing a correlation to any possible ways you've tried to compensate for deficits in the vats on the left (see page 79 in *Soul Healing* for an example).

In the book we also see that if we don't know what's going on, we'll try to fill our emptiest spaces with other people or things. What are some examples of how you might have done this in your own life?

On page 81, Tammy writes, "Please continue to dialogue with the Lord, asking the Holy Spirit to speak personally to you as you read this information, that you might sense His deeper work in you, whether it be from these words, or where He takes your thoughts in reaction to them." Take time to write to the Lord about this here.

Resolve

What do you think about the phrase on page 83, "unfulfilled longings create an internal cry for satisfaction"?

What is your emotional reaction to the reality that "hell is attempting to leverage against us whatever pain we have encountered to render us handicapped from living free, open, giving, risking, and trusting lives for the cause of Jesus Christ"? (p 86)

Praise the Lord for His faithful perseverance in our lives that He works in us "to will and to act according to His good purpose." (Philippians 2:13) Our exploration in this chapter is only a building block for the final dwelling you will be for God's full glory to rest in. So, we have needed to discover weak, compromised, and broken areas in order to apply the correct solution. If we refuse to face our internal damage, the dysfunctional patterns set in motion to handle it will continue. Instead of healing, the wound will continue to be exacerbated.

When we move through this portion of the journey, we need to file what we've learned close by so as not to forget what we now know about our urges and motivations. However, it is not our place to linger, lest we become self-consumed in some victim, immature, stance of "woe is me." To do so would be to thwart the bigger and better plan of our true Father. In Him, we see that "no matter how we have acquired our wounds, we all need the good news of the healing power of redemption: Evil meant our suffering for our destruction, but God meant it for our good."[7]

Dan Allender says the blessing of following this path to full restoration in Christ is: "the capacity to savor greater joy in spite of inevitable sorrow. We can dance, eat, sing, drink, talk, and party with more joy if our hearts truly grasp God's perspective on our past, the purpose of our future, and the passion we are to embrace in our present."[8]

The ransomed of the Lord will return. They will enter Zion with singing; everlasting joy will crown their heads. Gladness and joy will overtake them, and sorrow and sighing will flee away.
Isaiah 35:10

The damage to the masterpiece is evident, but so is the beauty underneath! Journey on!

> "We are never more alive to life than when it hurts – more aware both of our own powerlessness to save ourselves and of at least the possibility of a power beyond ourselves to save us and heal us if we can only open ourselves to it."
> Frederick Buechner

What truths do I feel God wanted me to receive in working through this chapter?

Eyes to See
Chapter Four

Refresh

Isn't it curious how popular shows like Antiques Roadshow have become? The allure of these simple programs is that common people bring in possessions to be evaluated for authenticity and value. The appraisal is done by an expert who can identify great works, even underneath layers of damage and aging. Viewers excitedly anticipate that plain looking piece which ends up being a famous artist's masterwork.

Like spiritual appraisers, the Trinity has proclaimed us priceless. No matter the level of distress or damage today, our underlying value is not in question. We must recognize damage for what it is – just damage. What is observable to the human eye is not the true value of something. The task at hand is assessing precisely what the level of harm is and proceeding with restoration.

The great news for us is that God specializes in resurrecting that which looks very far gone.

The prophet Ezekiel experienced this attribute of the Lord by way of a powerful vision. God showed him a valley full of very dry bones and asked him if he thought they could live again. Ezekiel answered, "O Sovereign Lord, you alone know." God told him to prophesy over them and – long story short – the bones started to rattle and, before his eyes, bodies were knit together. Ezekiel was standing before an apparent valley of death filled with life.

This is what the Sovereign Lord says: O my people, I am going to open your graves and bring you up from them; I will bring you back to the land of Israel. Ezekiel 37:12

How exciting for us that we are more than the sum total of our hurts and wounds. If we cooperate with God's Spirit, we will find that there is no corner of our soul that cannot be redeemed. In this chapter, as we search ourselves for what level of damage we have suffered, there is no greater promise than to realize all of heaven is committed to repairing each and every scratch, rip, divot, and tear of the masterpiece He created in us. Give Him praise!

We are hard pressed on every side, but not crushed; perplexed, but not in despair; persecuted, but not abandoned; struck down, but not destroyed. We always carry around in our body the death of Jesus, so that the life of Jesus may also be revealed in our body.
2 Corinthians 4:8-10

Reflect

Throughout this work it is critical to remember that the purpose of navigating our way through effects of wounds is:

____(p 89).

God wants us to be victors, not victims... to overcome, not to be overwhelmed.

William Arthur Ward 

Proverbs 23:7 says, "For as he thinks in his heart, so is he" (NKJV). Practical life bears this out. You could do an experiment for 30 days by thinking each day, "I might be getting depressed. I think I'm slipping into the blues." It's guaranteed you would be struggling with depression in a hurry. This reality can't be underestimated. If you believe you are second-rate, you'll act it. If you think you are an outcast, you'll end up being one. Conversely, if you view yourself as God's elect, being conformed to the image of Christ every day you walk this earth, then you'll act like someone humble, full of hope, and peacefully content.

How do you generally tend to think about yourself deep inside?

Our loving Father provides three sources of light for guiding us into Truth. They are:

The ________ of God, the ________ of God, and the ________ of God.
(refer to page 95)

What practices can you develop to better benefit from these sources God has provided? Be as specific as you can.

Think of someone you know that seems free... a person comfortable in their skin. In what ways do you see that freedom? What do you like about him/her?

Galatians 5:1 says, "It is for __________ that Christ set us free." What is an implication of that truth in your life?

In Psalm 139, David asks, "Search me, O God, and know my heart..." We are wise to ask Him to do this as well. Write a prayer, asking Him to speak to you, giving you eyes to see where you have been living out of your wounds and where you have distorted lenses in place. The Holy Spirit is the best source to give us eyes to see. Thank Him for His presence and pray for His wisdom. He will give it!

If any of you lacks wisdom, he should ask God, who gives generously to all without finding fault, and it will be given to him.
James 1:5

In the section, "Distorted Spectacles," Tammy explains how unrecognized lies can become a lens through which we perceive our lives. Describe in your own words how a lie can become like a pair of glasses we wear and view all of life through.

What are some examples of how these lies become lenses?

What is God bringing to your mind about a lens that you could be wearing?

So we fix our eyes not on what is seen, but on what is unseen. For what is seen is temporary, but what is unseen is eternal.
2 Corinthians 4:18

The seven indicators that someone could be living from wounds of omission (or trying to get empty buckets filled) are:

1. unable to be satisfied or constant discontentment – constant dissatisfaction or pervasive disappointment

2. trying to get too much, or more than another can give, out of already good relationships

3. experiencing the same type of hurt over and over again, almost as if you have a sign on your forehead

4. overreacting or being upset by things out of proportion to what the actual incident was and/or being oversensitive to certain types of people

5. despising or deadening deeper longings (or desires)

6. feeling very young on the inside (have an emotional age younger than your actual age)

7. being addicted or enslaved to something (and it can be anything)

Of these seven signs, do any resonate with you? Do you see yourself in any of these mirrors?

Describe how you see yourself in one or two of the seven patterns listed. It might be helpful to think about these two questions:

1. The idea of being "plucked" conveys that we are being oversensitive or overreacting to something. Can you think of what "plucks" you?

2. How old would you say you feel inside? Remembering that it's a shadow of a place we got stuck emotionally, can you think more about why you might choose this age for yourself?

The good news about Jesus living in us by His spirit is explained in Romans 6:5-8:

"If we have been united with him like this in his death, we will certainly also be united with him in his resurrection. For we know that our old self was crucified with him so that the body of sin might be done away with, that we should no longer be slaves to sin-because anyone who has died has been freed from sin. Now if we died with Christ, we believe that we will also live with him."

Rewrite this passage in your own words using "I" instead of "we."

What comes to your mind when you think of the word "shame?"

What does evil try to get us to believe through feelings of shame?

How has shame affected you?

Instead of shame, what is the truth about God and you?

Therefore, there is now no condemnation for those who are in Christ Jesus.
Romans 8:1

Have you ever thought that maybe the reason you have been hurt so badly is because you sought from man what only God could give?

Am I now trying to win the approval of men, or of God? Or am I trying to please men? If I were still trying to please men, I would not be a servant of Christ.
Galatians 1:10

Resolve

Consider this befitting conclusion to the hard work you did in this chapter:

> "Damage need not destroy us! The journey of life need not strip us of joy! The walk through the desert and the valley can actually redeem us – but not if our commitment is to flee from it. We live in a culture that is committed to escaping the veil of sorrow, but if we are willing to embrace the damage we can be saved."
>
> Dan Allender

God blesses those who ask for His wisdom, His perspective, His strength, His peace, and His glory. You can be surer of this than the chair you sit on. He is the one who provides over and above what we need.

Tammy concludes, "God has a plan to glorify Himself through your life and person, a plan that is an amazing, fulfilling path of maturity, freedom, and victory in Jesus." (p. 115)

Therefore, *"...let us throw off everything that hinders and the sin that so easily entangles, and let us run with perseverance the race marked out for us." Hebrews 12:1b*

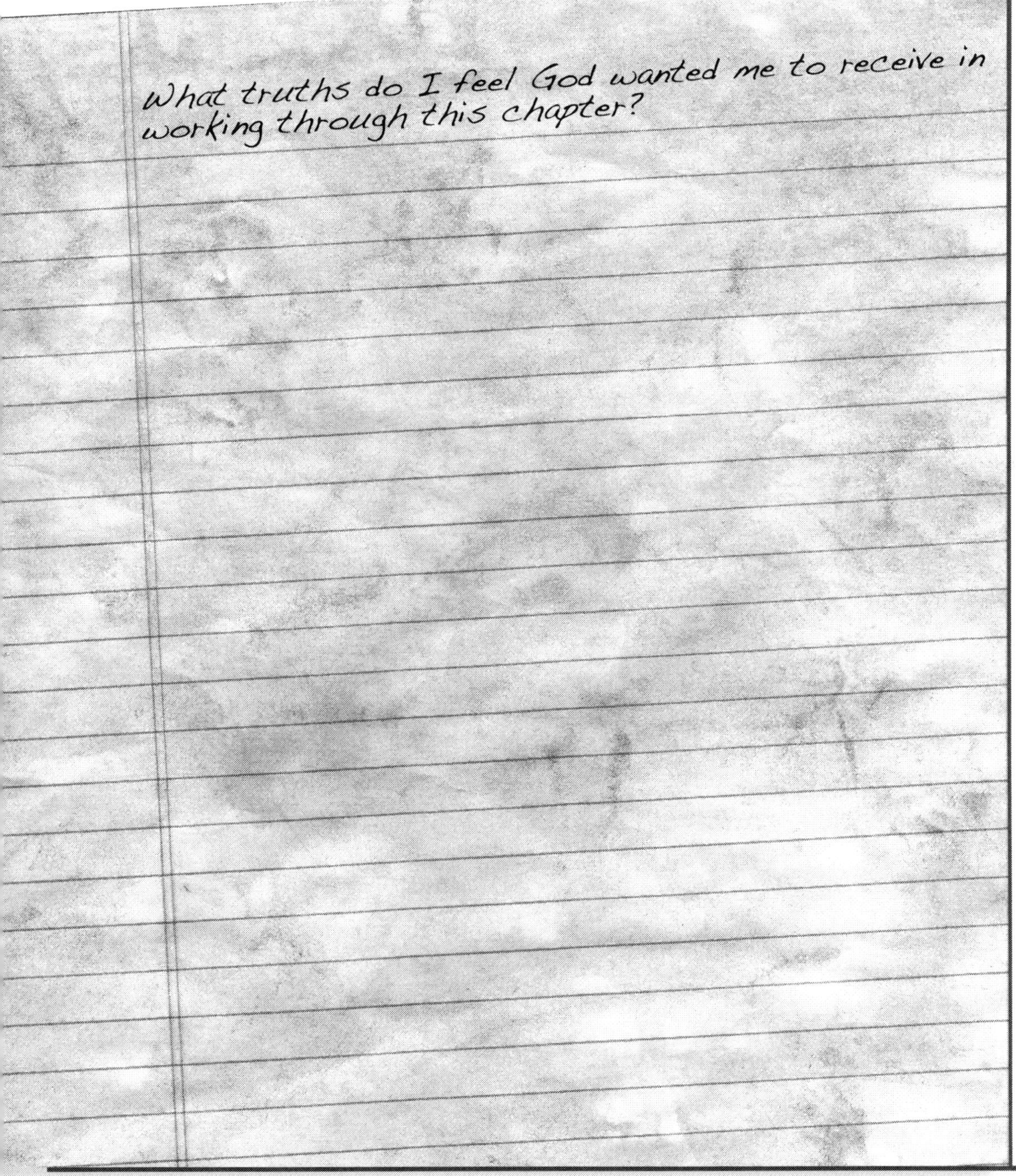

Real Filling
Chapter Five

Refresh

Behind-the-scenes commentary has been an enlightening trend in movie-making and watching. From earliest concept sketches to the costuming minutia, from the painstaking decisions for what scene needs cut to tough casting calls, we have come to appreciate the true works of art some epic movies are. Little did we know that it took a week to mold a nose for a creepy creature, or 15 hours to get into makeup, or that a certain scene could only be filmed at 2:00 AM during the full moon to get just the right lighting. And we can scarcely imagine that it took four years to finish. We wouldn't know any of that if the filmmakers hadn't clued us in. We might have just haphazardly watched it as something to relax us as we drifted off to sleep.

In any work of art, only the creator- the one through whom the beauty was captured and communicated - knows the nitty-gritty details of it. Only the artist knows how expensive that one wisp of texture was or how many "takes" it took to get the perfect cinematic moment. Only the sculptor knows precisely which clay matter is perfect for the vision he or she has. The creator of a masterpiece alone knows how to best care for, display, and protect it.

For we are God's workmanship, created in Christ Jesus to do good works, which God prepared in advance for us to do.
Ephesians 2:10

The bottom line for us is that only in the hands of the creator is a masterwork truly safe. Other people just don't know how to appreciate what this handiwork is about, how intricately crafted it is, and the power and potential it holds to captivate people's attention. They can try hard, but they can never be as in love with, as careful with, and as intimate with it as the architect is.

The Lord your God is with you, he is mighty to save. He will take great delight in you, he will quiet you with his love, he will rejoice over you with singing.
Zephaniah 3:17

This is directly parallel to our lives as children of the Most High God. We will never be appreciated, valued, loved, admired, cared for, and protected to the utmost by anyone except Jesus. Only our Creator knows how to display us properly, care for us best, and value us most. Other people, try as hard as they might, can never appreciate, love, and regard us for the intricately-woven, purposely-chosen, made-to-specification masterpiece that we are.

No one will handle you perfectly. You are loved to your absolute core and delighted in beyond comprehension by the One who created you and seeks to display the perfection of His Son through the awe-inspiring vessel of you.

For the Lord takes delight in his people.
Psalm 149: 4

Perhaps this awareness in and of itself will promote healing in our hearts that have too long been disappointed, disillusioned, and dismayed by the careless or harmful ways others have handled us.

Reflect

At the beginning of this chapter, we turn squarely to where the work and the person of Jesus fits into our past wounds and deficits. While it is true that Christ has conquered death and provided victory, it is not true that He will fill ______________________________ (see page 117).

Write this same thing again using your own words.

For you created my inmost being; you knit me together in my mother's womb. I praise you because I am fearfully and wonderfully made; your works are wonderful, I know that full well.
Psalm 139:13-14

Instead, what is God's agenda for our life's hurt and pain?

Describe what you see in diagram 5 on page 118--the false Christian view.

Then describe what you see on page 120 on diagram 6—the healthy Christian concept.

> “ When you and I are related to Jesus Christ, our strength and wisdom and peace and joy and love and hope may run out, but His life rushes in to keep us filled to the brim. We are showered with blessings, not because of anything we have or have not done, but simply because of Him.
>
> Anne Graham Lotz

According to Philippians 4:19, how is God providing for our needs?

How many needs is He providing for?

If so, then why do we so often fail to see how He is doing this in our own lives?

Delight yourself also in the Lord, and He will give you the desires and secret petitions of your heart.

Psalm 37:4 (Amplified)

In the vat diagram below, list as many characteristics of God you can think of based on the Scriptures provided and any others that come to mind.

Hosea 14:9
1 Corinthians 1:25
Jeremiah 10:10
Romans 8:15
Hebrews 13:5
Luke 1:37
Psalm 9:8
Psalm 145:13b

1 Chronicles 29:11-13
Deuteronomy 32:4
Numbers 23:19
1 Samuel 15:29
Daniel 2:22
1 Samuel 2:3
2 Timothy 2:13
1 John 1:9

Exodus 15:11
Psalm 99:9
Psalm 33:5
Nahum 1:7
Isaiah 63:7
Job 37:16
2 Thessalonians 3:3
Psalm 51:1

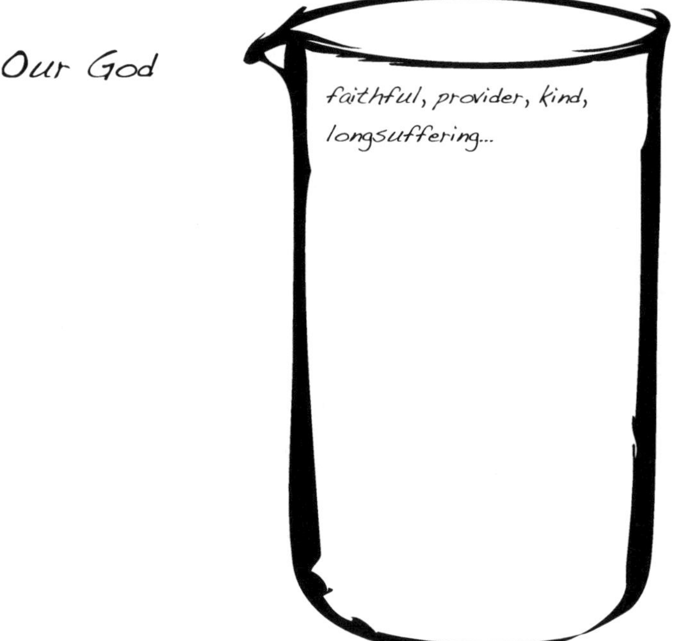

Hopefully, by now, you believe that God wants you to experience His joy and abundance. However, we must never forget that God is the consummate gentleman. He will not force His joy upon you; you must claim it for yourselves. This is where many of us get stuck. Tammy says we must apprehend the truth, embrace Christ, turn our eyes on Jesus. There's the clear idea that we have to reach out and take this gift of fullness as our own.

Talk about this in your own life – what is in your way, how this has "worked" when you have done it, how your life is different when you do turn to Christ, what God is encouraging you to do...

God is always there, working and moving, so our work is to fend off satan and tenaciously perceive our good God in everyday life. What instruction do the following verses give us for how to fight lies and see God in our lives?

Verse	What it tells us about fighting lies and seeing God
Let us then approach the throne of grace with confidence, so that we may receive mercy and find grace to help us in our time of need. (Hebrews 4:16)	
Let us fix our eyes on Jesus, the author and perfecter of our faith, who for the joy set before him endured the cross, scorning its shame, and sat down at the right hand of the throne of God (Hebrews 12:2).	
Brothers, I do not consider myself yet to have taken hold of it. But one thing I do: Forgetting what is behind and straining toward what is ahead (Philippians 3:13)	
We are hard pressed on every side, but not crushed; perplexed, but not in despair, persecuted, but not abandoned; struck down, but not destroyed. (2 Corinthians 4:8-9)	

How can our wounds cause us to view God like Santa Claus or a vending machine?

According to page 129, nothing will work to give us real change unless we believe what?

> "Our hearts are not healthy until they have been satisfied by the only completely healthy love that exists: the love of God Himself.
>
> Oswald Chambers"

This next section will require you to spend some time studying and processing. Plan now to camp here for a little while, remembering that the goal is a healed heart and changed life, not to get through this study guide as quickly as possible. While it's true that this is a lot of Scripture to look up, take to heart the truth of Isaiah 55:11: no word of God will return void. So, any and all time you spend looking at these will come back in a greater investment. His word is like yeast and when we put even just a little in us, it will grow and grow! Ultimately, while there is benefit to other good gifts God gives us (like talking to a friend, reading books, making food, checking Facebook and surfing the web), ingesting Scripture is the only thing guaranteed to have a multiplying effect in our souls.

Look at each of the Scriptures that follow. Describe below which ones God uses to touch your soul with His hope.

Proverbs 18:24
Hebrews 13:5
Romans 8:1
Romans 8:15
Romans 8:21
2 Corinthians 3:17
Galatians 5:1
Psalm 34:4
Romans 8:17
Romans 8:23
Romans 8:28
Jeremiah 31:3
Romans 8:39
Ephesians 3:20

 God is always far more willing to give us good things than we are anxious to have them.

Catherine Marshall 

Reflect

The redemptive, absolute, all-consuming love of God expressed and manifested in the fullness of the Lord Jesus Christ is complete. Said another way, it's enough. The love of Jesus is big enough to meet our every need, provide for our every longing, and satiate our deepest desires.

No conversation about Jesus and healing would be complete, however, without a reminder of God's redemptive purpose through pain. One passage which reflects such truth is Joel 2:25:

"I will repay you for the years the locusts have eaten."

This verse is hopeful in and of itself, but there's a beautiful intersection of the work you are doing in this chapter and the verse preceding this promise. Joel 2:24 says,

"The threshing floors will be filled with grain; ***the vats will overflow with new wine and oil****."*

A reference to "vats" in the holy Word of God! While we assess levels of deficit in earthly "vats," God is reminding us that His "vat" of love for us will be filled to the overflowing! The place of previous pain – "the years the locusts have eaten" – will be spilling over with new hope, strength, and joy! How awesome is that!

The allusions to new wine and oil in Scripture are incredibly rich – so much so that we can't capture it all here. However, oil symbolically refers to the Holy Spirit and new wine represents the gospel, or Jesus. Basically, what we have laid out for us in this Joel passage is a picture for our promise of healing. One thing happens, then the next, then the next.

First, we are called to repent: This means to change direction from what lies we have believed, what patterns we have developed, and sins of self-protection from being hurt. ("Rend your heart." Joel 2:13)

Then, the vats will overflow with new wine and oil: This means the fullness of Jesus Christ will indwell us completely. (Joel 2:24)

And from that truth, we will be repaid for the years the locusts have eaten: The place of previous pain will now be filled with joy, victory, faith, hope and love!! (Joel 2:25)

The new wine – the fullness of Jesus – can't be put into our old wineskins! Matthew 9:17 tells us if we try to pour new wine into old wineskins, they will be ruined. We cannot experience the full victory and healing of Jesus if we are trying to put Him in old places of hurt and pain. We can't try to shove the Lord into our deficits. (Recall the False Christian View diagram on page 118 of *Soul Healing*.) Instead, we must turn to God and allow Jesus to give us the fullness of Himself, not just some small idea of what we'd like Him to fix inside us. (Refer to the Healthy Christian View diagram on page 120.)

How incredibly sweet that God tells us our vats will be filled with the new wine and oil of Jesus Christ, and in finding fulfillment in Him, the years that evil sought to steal from us will be restored, and our souls will be refreshed.

"We do not need to beg Him to bless us; He simply cannot help it."
Hannah Whitall Smith

What truths do I feel God wanted me to receive in working through this chapter?

Space in Your Soul
Chapter Six

Refresh

When iPods were new and all the rage, my young son wanted one. We felt he was too young to have something that extravagant (read "expensive"). However, we did end up buying him another type of MP3 player for much less, and it was his first real piece of techno gear. He discovered a new aspect of himself through it, so he loved it. He was constantly tinkering with it.

Well, one day this beloved item was accidentally washed along with his laundry. It was devastating to him! The idea of simply going out and buying another was unthinkable because of all the time and effort he had put into making it just right. After lots of crying and upset, we took a corporate deep breath and began the arduous process of bringing it back to "life." It entailed drying, jeweler's screwdrivers, miniscule screws, paper-thin wires, surgeon's hands, and prayer. It even involved a grandpa who is an electrical engineer. All along, there were tears. Even we adults were skeptical a $35 piece of electronics could survive. Imagine the joy when the screen flickered on after it had been soaked in water and laid out in tiny pieces!

The hardest thing about the process was how the realization of my son's losses came in waves. At first he was just devastated by the overall fact that it was gone. Then, as we tried to repair it, he would remember a song on it which had taken him forever to find or how many hours it had taken his young fingers to type the album titles or how the CD from which he had copied a song had broken or a memory he and a friend made with it. It was as if, with each realization, the loss got worse. In actuality, though, that kind of assessment translated into more effort for this treasure to be restored.

The Spirit searches all things, even the deep things of God. For who among men knows the thoughts of a man except the man's spirit within him?
1 Corinthians 2:10, 11a

Hopefully, you're ahead of me here, and can see where we're going. We, as God's masterpieces, have a similar process to undergo. We will never engage in the depth of effort that it takes to bring our beautiful souls "back to life" if we do not allow ourselves to see the depth of loss. We must accept our wounds fully, lay them all out, grieve them, see the loss... so we can be fully healed! If a surgeon leaves a piece of gauze behind after an appendectomy, the patient can die. If a doctor gets "most" of the cancerous tumor out with some left behind, hope for healing is gone.

Oh, Lord, you have searched me, you and you know me.
Psalm 139:1

The God who has purchased your salvation with His blood, given you total victory, and who calls you to trust Him with all that you find in your soul, will fulfill His promise as you open yourself fully to His searching love.

Reflect

After we have become aware of our hurts, issues, sensitivities, wounds, patterns, filters, etc., we must take ownership of all this damage in order to walk in healing. What does it mean to take ownership of something?

Where are you, honestly, in the process of ownership and acceptance?

Even Jesus demonstrated how hard it is to accept pain and suffering at the hands of others. When His end was near, He prayed, "My Father, if it is possible, may this cup be taken from me. Yet not as I will, but as you will" (Matthew 26:39). We see clearly His grief and pain, then His acceptance. He took ownership of the hurt others had done and were about to do to Him.

Following Jesus' example for me means...

Lord, though it's hard, I now accept responsibility for ________________________

For better or for worse, what are some things your past has handed you?

Have you ever really entertained how you and your life would be different were it not for your wounds and their effects?

Who do you think you would've been if unaffected by life's hurts?

What is your understanding of grief?

Are you grieving anything right now?

Where are you in the process? Are you acknowledging the grief or are you numb to it, shutting it off, keeping busy, etc.?

In your anger do not sin; when you are on your beds, search your hearts and be silent.

Psalm 4:4

Provide your reaction to this statement: "Anger is actually like a blanket, and almost always, hurt is what is being covered."

Grief is the reaction to any loss. What are some examples of losses, even ones we don't typically associate with grieving?

An interesting facet to grieving is captured in a client's observation: "Grief is like a bunch of ribbons all tied together. When you pull up one loss, it's like they all come up together." This is the reason many people won't "go there" with sadness and loss – they are afraid it will overwhelm them. But, we have to discipline our souls to remember we can trust God. He longs to be gracious to us, show us compassion, and love us. His will for our restoration does include the hard process of grieving, but He will be with us, giving peace and comfort even in the midst of the hardest times.

> For every stream of grief that flows into our lives there is a deeper river of peace that comes from the Holy Spirit.
>
> Jim Cymbala

What are we forgetting about God when we blame Him as uninvolved or unconcerned when it comes to how humans hurt each other (see page 141)?

The concept of an "armoire" is used to describe how we shove away hurts without really dealing with them.

How "full" would you say your internal "armoire" is?

What do you think it is full of?

What is the danger in living the "push the thing down" way?

What does it mean that grief generally comes in waves?

How can living life with an internal armoire full of hurt, pain, and sadness be self-indulgent?

Use this chart to help you identify grief in your own life.

Losses in my life	Grieved/not grieved	What it has looked like
Miscarriage	grieved	lots of tears
Poor relationship with Mom growing up	not grieved	I resent her
Spouse views pornography	not grieved	I keep very, very busy
Unable to have children	grieved	lots of creative writing and spending time with other families

How have you seen the principle of "what's in the dark grows, what's in the light shrinks," in your own life?

What is something (and it can be anything) inside you that has too much power, is taking up too much space, or that is controlling you somehow that needs to come out?

On page 158, it says, "Becoming familiar with our inner thirst is excellent, because this very desire can drive us to deeper intimacy with the Lord···In short, nothing can satisfy our deepest hunger except the sort of relationship that only God offers." How does this speak to you?

When you think about your relationship with the Lord right now, where would you place yourself on this continuum?

1	5	10
feeling disconnected from the Lord	a little bit connected	deep, abiding, intimate relationship with the Lord

How might acceptance, ownership, and grieving affect your feeling of connectedness with the Lord?

Resolve

Surely he took up our infirmities and carried our sorrows, yet we considered him stricken by God, smitten by him, and afflicted. But he was pierced for our transgressions, he was crushed for our iniquities; the punishment that brought us peace was upon him, and by his wounds we are healed. Isaiah 53:4, 5

By His wounds we are healed. It is pure grief that Jesus had to die for my sins. It is through this pure grief that we are healed. However, we are not saved or healed if we don't first accept this painful wound – Christ was pierced, spat upon, killed ruthlessly while being laughed at. If we don't accept this wound fully for what it is, and take the truth of it into our own souls, we will not be saved. The Word says "that if you confess with your mouth, 'Jesus is Lord,' and believe in your heart···then you will be saved" (Romans 10:9). We can't just know He is God, we must ingest it into our belief systems as a part of us.

For me to live is Christ and to die is gain.
Philippians 1:21

You see, religion keeps the horror of it all at a distance. There are pretty crucifixes in gold, stunning stained glass windows, and robes of velvet. The religious folk of Jesus' day, the Pharisees, confessed with their mouths, but did they believe in their hearts? No. When we pull Jesus close in – like the woman kissing his feet, like John laying on his breast, like John the Baptist drawing attention away from himself and putting it on Jesus, like Thomas asking to touch his scarred hands – we are demonstrating true belief (Luke 7:36-50, John 13:23 [NASB], Matthew 3:1-13, John 20:27-29). Watching the movie The Passion was gut-wrenching, and yet drew me nearer. The more we allow the depth of this injustice and its grief to rest on us, the more we live in strength and passion – with intensity and purpose.

I want to know Christ and the power of his resurrection and the fellowship of sharing in his sufferings, becoming like him in his death, and so, somehow, to attain to the resurrection from the dead.
Philippians 3:10, 11

Conversely, distant interaction with God says, "I'm pretty sure Jesus died and rose again and that this is the way for the salvation of my soul, so I want to be sure to do what's right by God." That's fire insurance, as a friend of mine says. Intimate interaction with Jesus says, "I stake my life on Jesus, and know I am dead in every way without him." The difference is subtle and yet massive. It's subtle because religious people look devout. They seem to believe. Do you seem to believe, or have you truly come to stake your whole self on Jesus?

Only people who fully pull the death and resurrection in all its gruesomeness close in to their chest and believe it deep within, can experience the full salvation and healing of Christ. The principle is this one: the emptier the cup, the more it can be filled up. The more we lay our "stuff" out, and go after anything in our souls that is hidden or secret, the more of Christ we can experience. His fullness is ours at the moment of repentance. Our experience of His totality within us is the issue. The uncleaned and ignored closets of our hearts get in the way of our full access to His healing.

Following the cup principle, when we accept and grieve our own pain, then healing occurs. If we keep it at a distance, we can get "some" healing. If our cup is a bit emptied, then a dose of freedom can be put in there. But when we empty it out, all that is in us – our memories, our sadnesses, our injustices, things done to us, things we've done to others – then our cup is empty enough for full, complete, and total healing.

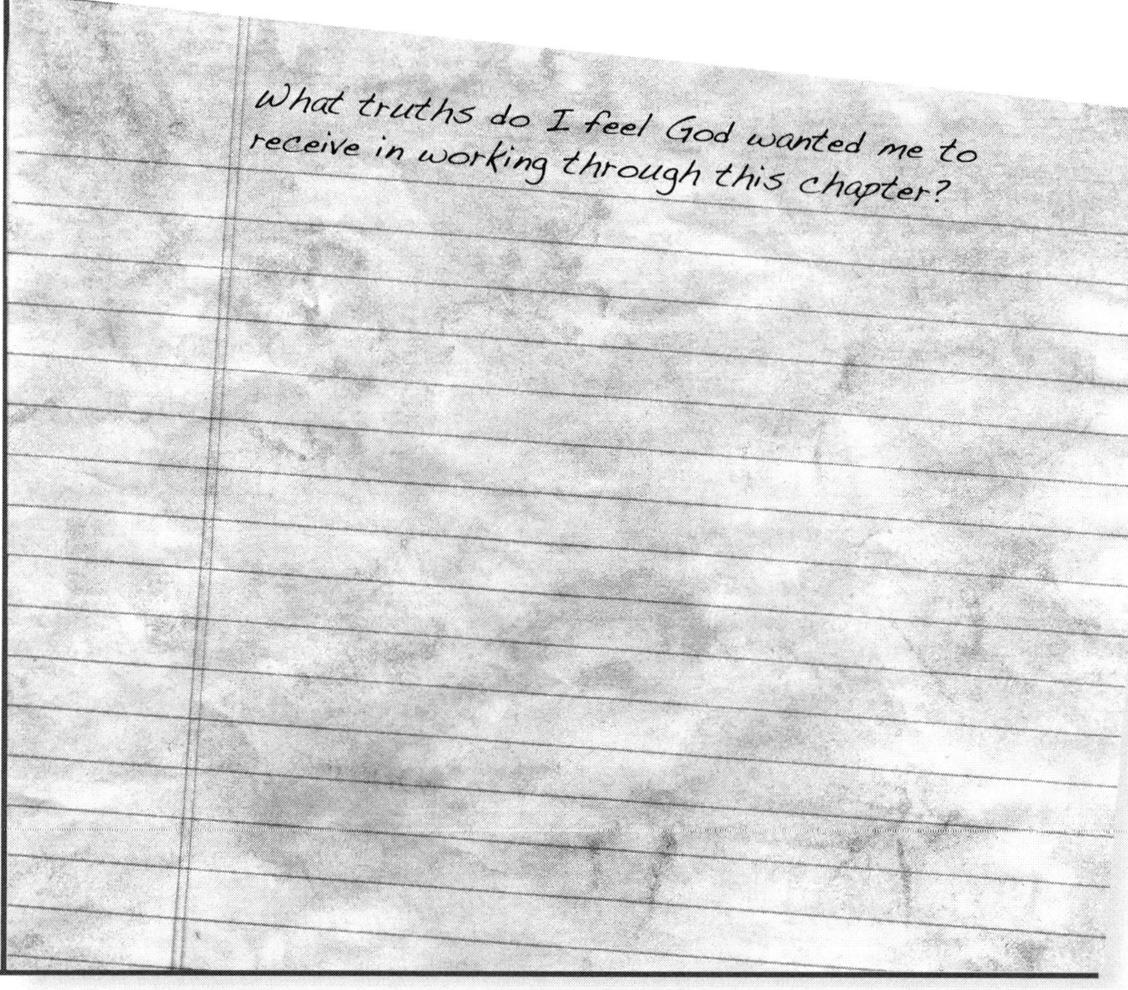

Hiding Out
Chapter Seven

Refresh

For years, art historians knew of a Van Gogh drawing, and always wondered if it was a sketch of a completed painting which existed somewhere. After decades of searching, the painting was discovered in a most unusual place -- concealed under another painting. It was revealed through an X-ray of another work. To expose this beautiful work, the painting over it would have to be destroyed.

What a poignant picture for us of…us! We are God's beautiful masterpiece, created in His image with an intended self perfectly suited for His purposes for us on this earth. Then we have experiences of hurt, pain, shame, betrayal, disappointment, abandonment, and regret, so we decide we must alter ourselves in some way for protection. With each situation, we cover over another area of ourselves until most of God's original work in us is hidden. People in our lives get a sense of who we are, like the Van Gogh sketch. They might even try to search to catch a glimpse of what they suspect might exist. However, until we are willing to destroy the masks, vows, addictions, and self-protective patterns in which we live, the true million-dollar work of art is obscured.

No one lights a lamp and puts it in a place where it will be hidden, or under a bowl. Instead, he puts it on its stand so that those who come in may see the light.
Luke 11:33

Staying with the analogy, God is giving us a therapeutic X-ray through this study guide. It is an amazing work of art, your soul, and it is not meant to be covered. Our purpose in doing the work required in this study guide is that the Spirit might empower us to walk in the truth of God's perspective of us, to reveal how we are not doing that, and to provide us new ways to live life in truth. The following chapters of this study guide provide many helpful tools for doing so. This present chapter, though, is fixated on helping to remove false fronts we have erected, walls we have whitewashed, and barriers we have hidden behind.

Reflect

What are vows?

What is the problem with or danger in making vows?

You are like whitewashed tombs, which look beautiful on the outside but on the inside are full of dead men's bones and everything unclean.
Matthew 23:27

Review the list of common vows on page 162. Which vow or vows in that list do you realize you might have made? List any others below as well that you think you could have made.

What are masks?

What do we use emotional masks to do?

> From the place of our woundedness we construct a false self. We find a few gifts that work for us, and we try to live off them. Stuart found he was good at math and science. He shut down his heart and spent all his energies perfecting his "Spock" persona. There, in the academy, he was safe; he was also recognized and rewarded. "When I was eight," confesses Brennan Manning, "the impostor, or false self, was born as a defense against pain. The impostor within whispered, 'Brennan, don't ever be your real self anymore because nobody likes you as you are. Invent a new self that everybody will admire and nobody will know.'" Notice the key phrase: "as a defense against pain," as a way of saving himself.
>
> John Eldredge

Which mask or masks do you think you sometimes wear to deflect people from seeing you? Circle the masks in the list below where you see yourself. Add any others you think you wear.

humor	super spiritual	constantly busy
lone ranger	aloof	depressed
quiet	know-it-all	turn-it-back-on-you
the "yes person"	have it all together	sarcasm
always serving	tough guy/girl	devil's advocate

Woe to you! For you are like concealed tombs, and the people who walk over them are unaware of it.
Luke 11:44 (NASB)

Think about and describe when, why, and how.

What are common ways people anesthetize themselves today?

What is the outcome of such habits of numbing?

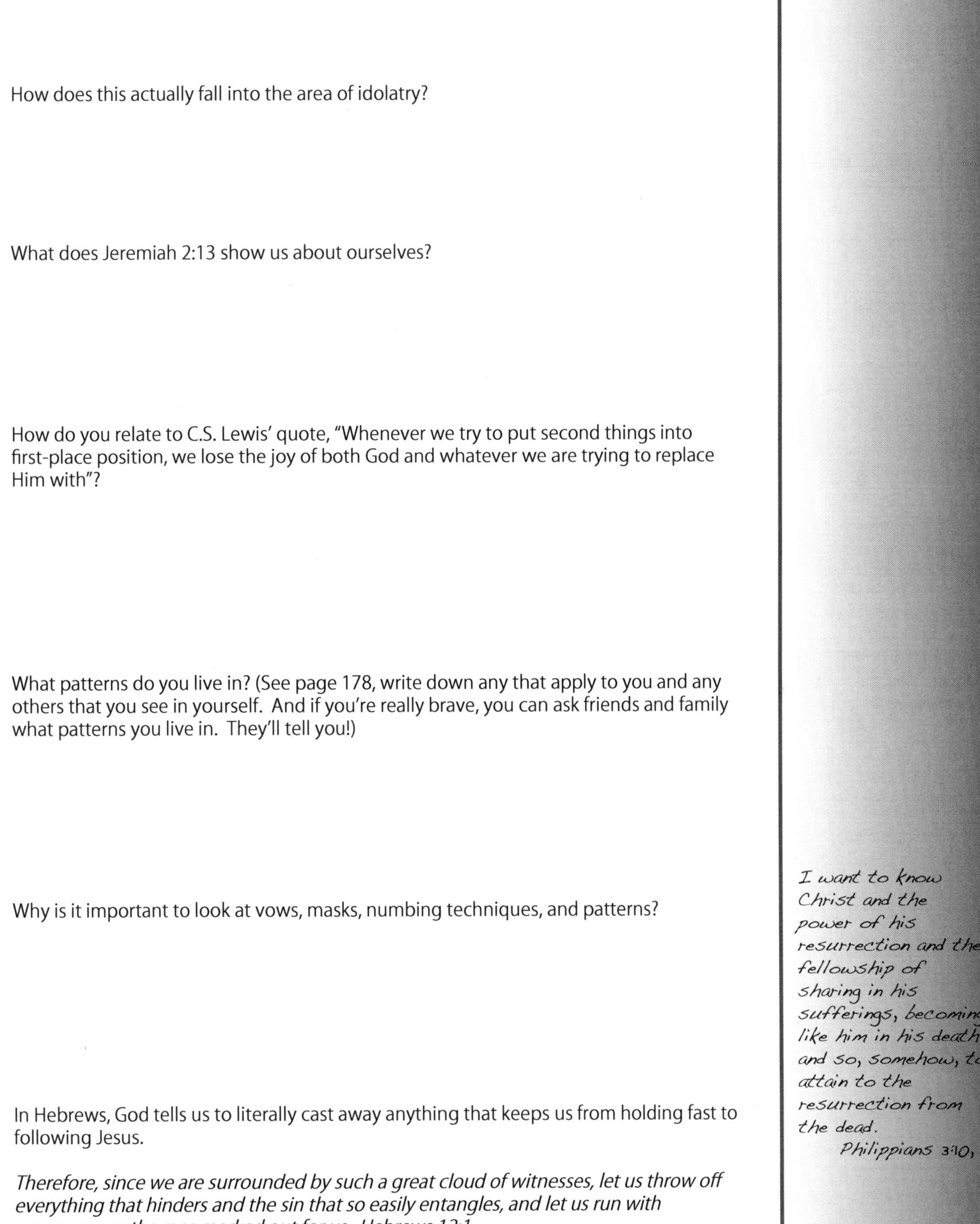

How does this actually fall into the area of idolatry?

What does Jeremiah 2:13 show us about ourselves?

How do you relate to C.S. Lewis' quote, "Whenever we try to put second things into first-place position, we lose the joy of both God and whatever we are trying to replace Him with"?

What patterns do you live in? (See page 178, write down any that apply to you and any others that you see in yourself. And if you're really brave, you can ask friends and family what patterns you live in. They'll tell you!)

Why is it important to look at vows, masks, numbing techniques, and patterns?

In Hebrews, God tells us to literally cast away anything that keeps us from holding fast to following Jesus.

Therefore, since we are surrounded by such a great cloud of witnesses, let us throw off everything that hinders and the sin that so easily entangles, and let us run with perseverance the race marked out for us. Hebrews 12:1

I want to know Christ and the power of his resurrection and the fellowship of sharing in his sufferings, becoming like him in his death, and so, somehow, to attain to the resurrection from the dead.
Philippians 3:10, 11

Following the outline of this verse, fill in whatever masks and patterns you have identified that are keeping you from persevering in faith, and prayerfully give those over once and for all:

I now, by faith in Jesus, who lives in me, lay aside ______________________________,
(masks)
and the ______________________________ which so easily entangles and I run
(patterns)
with endurance the race that is set before me (Hebrews 12:1).

Vows, since they came about willfully, must be undone by an act of our will. There may or may not be feelings which accompany this act, but it does need to be a clear cut movement of the will. Revoke any intentional or even unintentional vows you may have discovered on your healing journey here:

I now take back the vow that I will never let people see the real me.

Lord, I am sorry I told You I'd never join a Bible study again. I revoke that vow now and put you back into your rightful place as Lord of all my life.

satan, I no longer agree with you that no one can be trusted.

If someone were to ask you, "Who is the real you?" what would you say? Really, what would you say? Would you describe your personality, what you do, or what others say you are like? What would be your grid for answering this question?

Many people who decry not having any friends who really know them, or hurt because it seems like after so many years a spouse just "doesn't understand me", don't realize they are the main culprit in this situation. All too frequently, we forget people can't read our minds. We forget how easily they are thrown off the scent of "the real us" if we look outwardly confident or aloof. We forget they have their own insecurities they are trying to see beyond and work through in relational interactions. So, we really can't blame them when we are wearing masks and living in protected patterns, then, can we? It's really not their fault when they treat us like we're okay when we keep acting like it, right?

Notice *Soul Healing* didn't start off with this chapter. It's because we can't hope to remove masks, revoke vows, and change deflecting patterns of living unless we know we are secure in God's great love for us. We can be our true selves only when we know that God sees our deepest selves and loves us more than we can comprehend.

The Real Me
By Natalie Grant

Foolish heart looks like we're here again
Same old game of plastic smile
Don't let anybody in
Hiding my heartache, will this glass house break
How much will they take before I'm empty
Do I let it show, does anybody know?

But you see the real me
Hiding in my skin, broken from within
Unveil me completely
I'm loosening my grasp
There's no need to mask my frailty
Cause you see the real me

Painted on, life is behind a mask
Self-inflicted circus clown
I'm tired of the song and dance
Living a charade, always on parade
What a mess I've made of my existence
But you love me even now
And still I see somehow

Wonderful, beautiful is what you see
When you look at me
You're turning the tattered fabric of my life into
A perfect tapestry

I just wanna be me
But you see the real me
Hiding in my skin, broken from within
Unveil me completely
I'm loosening my grasp
There's no need to mask my frailty
Cause you see the real me
And you love me just as I am
Wonderful, beautiful is what you see
When you look at me

What truths do I feel God wanted me to receive in working through this chapter?

Did not the one who made the outside make the inside also?
Luke 11: 40b

Hallelujah, God's treasure in you has been recovered! Restored! Reinstated! Rather than some garage-worthy cast-off, you are in actuality a masterpiece of great value. It's true that God specifically created you with someone in mind. Not the "you" of this moment, but the "you" from His view, through the overlay of Christ and with eternity in view. He will not be thwarted in His plan for your intended self. Again, hallelujah!

By now in your journey of soul healing, you have understood your value as His creation, learned about the intricate nature of what He has intended for your life, discovered there is a ferocious battle for ownership of you, and exposed a targeted attempt to destroy you. You have seen ways in which you distort, devalue, and cover over His glory in your life. Much has come clear in terms of why you do the things you do, how you got to be the "you" of today, and what recovery work needs done.

From this clarity, we move into a section focused on equipping you to rightly handle and care for God's work of you. The next four chapters in particular concentrate on providing a toolbox of strategies, skills, and perspectives designed to rightly handle God's purpose of your life. The initial chapters provided a foundation, fixing what was wrong with it, and now we move into building solidly and confidently on it. It's time to powerfully cooperate with the deep work of God in and through our lives!

Everyone who hears these words of mine and puts them into practice is like a wise man who built his house on the rock. Matthew 7:24

In our continuing work, just like in our everyday lives, we have got to remember that evil is still bent on marring, maiming, and murdering us. So, don't be surprised when you take a step toward health and it doesn't go well. Don't be discouraged when you practice a new discipline and feel unsuccessful. Don't be overcome when you take a risk and it fails. That's what growth and change look like at first. It's because hell wants you to stay put and not move forward! You can't ever forget the unseen wagering that occurs over you. (If you've never read *Piercing the Darkness* by Frank Peretti, now might be the time to do so.) It's particularly rewarding to think about how evil, by its very willingness to fight so hard to hurt you, inadvertently affirms your high value to the kingdom of God.

An excellent depiction of this reality is captured by C. S. Lewis in *The Screwtape Letters*. In it, he brilliantly exposes the systematic and sinister approach of evil towards God's chosen children. Spiritual battle is revealed as a specifically designed scheme against each Christ follower. The intention is to derail and distract Christians from their faith any way possible, which is usually through the subtleties of life as opposed to overt attacks. Lewis depicts this diabolical plotting between two hellish minions, one apparently a mentor who is writing to another in training. Here is one such transaction (remembering that the "Enemy" is actually referring to God):

"But do remember, the only thing that matters is the extent to which you separate the man from the Enemy. It does not matter how small the sins are, provided that their cumulative effect is to edge the man away from the Light and out into the Nothing. Murder is no better than cards if cards can do the trick. Indeed, the safest road to Hell is the gradual one – the gentle slope, soft underfoot, without sudden turnings, without milestones, without signposts."[9]

So, in as many ways as possible and as subtly as possible, evil is constantly trying to shift our focus. Anything to keep us from remembering God is altogether good. Everything to keep us from remembering we are infinitely special to God. When we lose this, we lose the battle.

And so with great energy and enthusiasm, let this additional Lewis quote propel us as we proceed with this life-altering work. The evil character advises:

"The great thing is to prevent his [the Christian's] doing anything. As long as he does not convert it into action, it does not matter how much he thinks about this new repentance... Let him, if he has any bent that way, write a book about it; that is often an excellent way of sterilizing the seeds which the Enemy plants in a human soul. Let him do anything but act. No amount of piety in his imagination and affections will harm us if we can keep it out of his will." (p. 57)[10]

Because He has set us free, let's **act**!!

I run in the path of your commands, for you have set my heart free. Psalm 119:32

Mental Healing (The Intellectual Pathway)
Chapter Eight

Refresh

You have taken off your old self with its practices and have put on the new self, which is being renewed in knowledge in the image of its Creator. Colossians 3:9-10

This chapter contains very practical strategies for how to live in the truth of Colossians 3:9-10 – how to take off our old selves and their practices. By doing so, we are cooperating with God, who is "re-creating His image in us, day by day and bit by bit. Romans 8:29 tells us that we are being conformed to the image of Christ, and Colossians 1:15 tells us that Christ is the image of God."[11] Through the incredible gift of the life of Christ implanted in us when we gave our lives to Him, God's image in us is being restored.

It's a process which takes time and requires perseverance and patience. But, we can have extreme confidence in this process because of the truth captured in Colossians 3:10 -- that we have actually exchanged an old for a new self. While it was a once-for-all transaction, the verb tense changes noticeably halfway through the verse. We have exchanged selves; we are being renewed. It's a fact – "the image of God in us is being restored as painstakingly as a Michelangelo masterpiece."[12]

Forgetting what is behind and straining toward what is ahead, I press on toward the goal to win the prize for which God has called me heavenward in Christ Jesus. All of us who are mature should take such a view of things.
Philippians 3:13b- 15a

Remind yourself frequently of this truth as you practice with the strategies, perspectives, and tools for change given in this chapter.

Be encouraged that this work of God will not be thwarted and keep pressing on toward that goal!!

Reflect

What do verses like Romans 12:2, 2 Corinthians 10:5, and Philippians 4:8 show us about the battleground in spiritual warfare?

If the true force of change is our will in cooperation with God's Spirit, what does this say to you about your feelings?

The primary tool for healing (when it comes to fighting lies and the damage evil sought to do through wounds) is to:

(1) Recognize

(2) Reject/Rebuke/Renounce/Resist

(3) Replace

Describe what each of these steps is about.

Actually refusing to allow lies to penetrate your mind is a critical part of walking in the healing truths of Jesus. We must reject vigorously anything contrary to God's character, Word, and ways. However, sometimes it is difficult to reject a lie because there is a modicum of truth contained in it. For instance, the lie might be: "People will always hurt me." That's hard to patently reject because others do hurt us. However, we still must reject what is untrue. Some people hurt us, others bless us, and God gives us others to love and to love us as a reflection of His Kingdom.

Another lie might be: "I am stupid." The truth could be that you are dyslexic, which doesn't have anything to do with intelligence. Further, it is God's design that different people have different types of intelligences, so if you don't have the type of "smarts" a friend does, this does not make you stupid. Finally, you are fearfully and wonderfully made by God, who is pleased with His creation of you.

Give an example of some lies you can think of that would be hard to reject because they contain a tiny bit of truth:

I must be unlovable because I don't get along with my mother-in-law. It's not true that I'm not lovable just because Tom's mom and I don't see eye to eye. God will continue His work in both of us!

What is the point of the diaper example on page 196?

It is sometimes helpful to recall significant shaping events in our lives to help us uncover the lies with which we struggle. Name two or three of your most vivid memories, even if they don't seem particularly big or hurtful, and think about what lies could have entered through those events.

Event	Possible Lies
Dad left when I was 8.	*I'm not important.* *It's my fault.* *People who say they'll be there for you can't be trusted.*
A friend gossiped about me.	*I'll always be betrayed.* *I am lesser than others.*

Spend some time now actually using your tool for truth and healing, using the grid below to help you take your thoughts captive (2 Corinthians 10:5):

What are some lies I routinely struggle with?	Rebuke, renounce, or resist them.	What is God's truth about me or this situation?
Recognize	Reject	Replace
I'm a bad wife	*In Jesus' name I rebuke the lie that I am a horrible wife*	*I am an imperfect person, but the perfect partner for my husband.*
I'm ugly	*I renounce the lie that I should feel unattractive because the blood of Jesus covers me.*	*I am beautifully and wonderfully made.*

Things will never get better	I rebuke hopelessness or any similar spirit in the name of Jesus	I can do all things through Christ who strengthens me, including working through this problem to see change.

You've probably realized by now that recognizing lies can be challenging. While some untruths are blatant and easy to spot, others can be very troublesome. Sometimes, because of how and when they come, accusations can feel so very true. Why does it seem some lies land so deep, as if evil can read our thoughts?

It is paramount to realize evil cannot read our minds. Pure malevolence cannot dwell inside a purified and holy temple of the Lord Jesus Christ. So, hellish spirits do not know our thoughts. However, they can read our actions, patterns, behaviors, and words.

A counselor trained in human behavior can tell a lot about a person simply by watching him or her and the familiarity that comes with knowing his or her life story. We can know Sara is angry when her neck starts to redden, or that John is sad when he switches the subject to sports. These become clear simply by observation over a period of time. Think about how long evil has been watching us and taking notes on our hurts, pains, injustices, betrayals, and fears. This is why the lies can be so hard to fight sometimes. We are so vulnerable to them and evil calculates just when is best to whisper them in our ears. It happens most often when we are tired, hungry, after a big victory or spiritual event, or often before a time of great effectiveness for the Lord.

No matter what, remember with confidence that satan cannot read your mind. Instead, the hellish hosts are trained in reading your non-verbals, coupled with the knowledge of your life's events. Don't give the enemy more power by believing or fearing differently. (Incidentally, this is just one more reason our speech is such a huge area we need to control. It is something "outside" of us – heard by both the physical and spiritual realms.)

What is your reaction to this thought?

What priority must God's Word have in our lives if we are to hope for true healing?

Hebrews 4:12 says God's Word is living and active. Those words give a sense of movement and energy. It's really helpful to think of every piece of Scripture like yeast growing in us. Yeast starts out incredibly small, and has a huge effect, especially as it is worked throughout dough. Just like that dough, if we put God's Word in our souls and knead it around, in a short amount of time this living and active substance will become huge inside us.

You can stake your life on this truth: Isaiah 55:11 says the Word of God won't ever come back empty. It can't return void. Every other "thing" we do will pale in comparison to the pulsating power of the Holy Word of God in our healing journey. Ingesting Scripture is a guaranteed vehicle of deep change within us. We must actually take it in, though. We have to swallow it, gulp it down, not just let it rest inside our mouths.

Do you have misperceptions or misconceptions about the Word of God that have been getting in the way of it being a more regular part of your daily life?

(Perhaps this is another opportunity to recognize, reject, and replace! Do so here if you recognize some hellish lie about your own interaction with God's Word.)

There are certainly many misconceptions about forgiveness that exist. One is that we get to the place where we can "feel good" about offering forgiveness to someone. Some people make the mistake of thinking that it's not painful to forgive. Well, Colossians 3 says to forgive as the Lord forgave. When we really think about that, how did the Lord forgive? What did it look like when Jesus forgave us?

He suffered excruciating pain, He bled, and He withstood the mockery of the ones He was forgiving. Can you even imagine looking at someone who has hurt you and telling him you forgive him while he mocks and sneers at you? Let's be straight-up about this. Forgiveness is hard. Painful. Requiring death to self. That's what the forgiveness of the Lord Jesus looked like. And we are to forgive like He did. So, be freed up from the thought that you have to feel godly or spiritual or kind or magnanimous before you forgive. You can choose to endure that pain right now, because you love Jesus so much and that's what He did for you.

What are some other common misconceptions about forgiveness?

What is your definition of forgiveness after considering this section?

Who is forgiveness for?

What are two helpful things to remember as we consider forgiveness (see page 203)?

> "Grudges are like hand grenades; it is wise to release them before they destroy you."
>
> Barbara Johnson.

Is there someone you need to forgive and will you do so now, for the sake of Jesus?

While not a formula, here is a helpful reminder that you are releasing a person back to God when you forgive:

"I now choose to release ______________ for doing ________________ to me, and I entrust you, Lord, with them and this situation."

> "Forgiveness is actually the best revenge because it not only sets us free from the person we forgive, but it frees us to move into all that God has in store for us."
>
> Stormie Omartian

In the section, "Playing Catch," we are reminded that paying attention to our thoughts and actions can help us change. On pages 206-212, what do you see that are some things you need to catch yourself doing?

What "little tests" do you put others through or have you yourself been put through?

- What do you know about your own sensitivities?
- Around whom am I on eggshells?
- What situations are terrible for me to be in?
- Why is it so bad for me?
- Where in life do I find evil having a heyday with me?

Why will we never be totally comfortable or at ease in this life?

How can this perspective on truth actually help us heal?

Consider this quote on page 218: "…the power of our will is huge, and can transform our entire existence. Notice I didn't say it could change our circumstances or the people around us. However, the extreme power of our will in submission to God for His plan and purposes is a life-altering truth."

In your most challenging struggle right now, how do you now see that you have the power of choice?

On pages 219-221, there are four critical choices listed. What are these choices we must make in the process of true healing?
1.
2.
3.
4.

Which of those speaks to you personally the most right now?

Resolve

Therefore, holy brothers, who share in the heavenly calling, fix your thoughts on Jesus... Hebrews 3:1

Sarah Young portrays God's thoughts communicated to us in the first person in her book *Dear Jesus*. These words capture well God's heart for us in the area of our primary battleground:

"Beloved, don't be surprised by the fierceness of the battle for your mind. The enemy and his evil army abhor your closeness to Me, so they send missiles of deception into your mind. Fixing your thoughts on Me will continue to be a struggle, because of this ongoing barrage of demonic interference. Another factor is your own fallen nature: Your mind did not escape the effects of the Fall.

Many things can affect your ability to think clearly – poor sleep, health, or nutrition: lack of fresh air and exercise, worries of the world, excessive busyness. Nonetheless, it is still possible to exert much control over your thinking. Ask My Spirit to help you in this endeavor. Don't simply let your thoughts run freely; set a guard over them. Be self-controlled and alert. When you become aware of hurtful or unholy thoughts, bring them to Me. Talk with Me about your struggles; choose to make your thoughts a conversation with Me. As you persevere in making good thought choices, you will enjoy my refreshing presence more and more."[13]

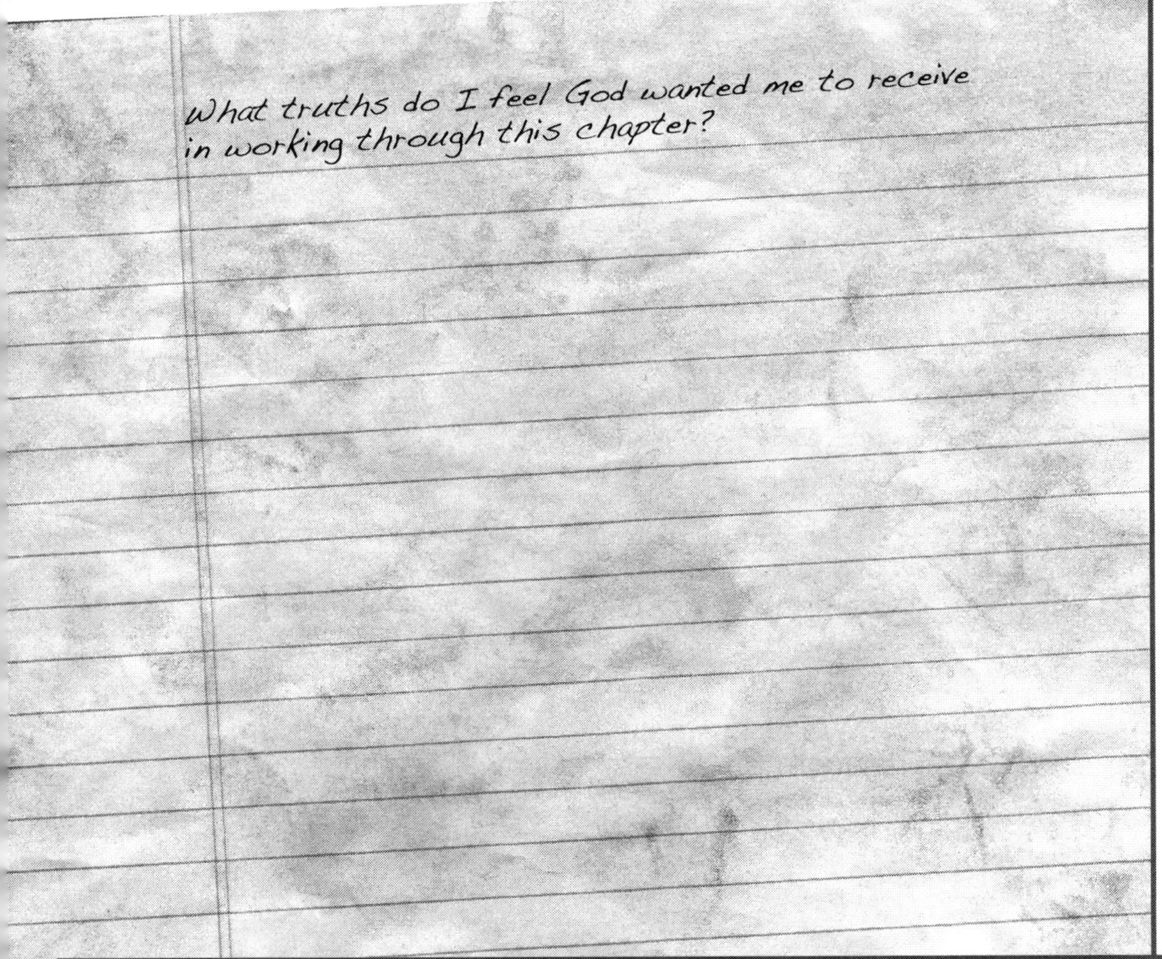

Real Healing

Real-life testimonies of people on the Soul Healing Journey

Max's Story

At thirty-three, I never expected to learn that I was physically and sexually abused at some point in my childhood. This blow rocked my foundation, but ironically, there was a part of me that was relieved because I had always thought there was something wrong with me. My world was cold, dark, and very, very lonely. I often felt trapped and emotionally drained. For awhile, I actually believed that is who God created me to be. Once I came to grips and accepted the reality of what had happened, my eyes were opened to something I had pretty much ignored: satan is my enemy and he is more active than I ever knew.

When my secrets were exposed, evil tried to use every past pain, hurt, and affliction as leverage to pry me away from the people that loved me as well as my Heavenly Father. I experienced physical and emotional ailments, and even times when darkness supernaturally threatened to overcome me. It became very clear that satan wasn't just trying to make me sin, but attempting to devour me, as 1 Peter 5:8 warns. He would have loved nothing more than for me to end my life on one of those numerous occasions when I was bombarded with feelings of desperation and despair, but God had different plans.

In my case, hell's message was, "At all costs, act like everything is ok. Don't think about what's happened and definitely don't let anyone else see your pain." But God was teaching me to battle lies, and to open my numb heart to His healing. I started unpacking my heart one piece at a time. The thoughts and feelings I had to relive were so hard. There were times when I felt totally naked. It would have been so much easier to continue the repression. But it was in those times when I saw and felt God the most. Thank God He provided me courage. If we don't face our wounds again with God as our guide, we will never truly be free. God was amazing in this process and He was right there with me, gently prodding and revealing information in amounts He knew I could handle. This was one of the first times in my life I truly opened up my heart and spirit to His love.

In this battle, one of the landmark decisions I made was to get baptized. This symbolized that I was claiming victory over evil and actively engaging the daily battle. I chose my side in this war. I wish I could say the pushback from the enemy subsided, but it didn't because this was an epic battle for my heart. Evil's foothold on me had prohibited me from experiencing Christ the way God intended.

God is continuing to teach me what the battle looks like. I believe the gauge is not necessarily how I *feel*, but how I *battle*. When satan attacks, do I push back or give in? It's not about feeling good all the time. It's all about winning the second by second battle against the lies from satan. Sure there will be hard days, but to know each day you are becoming more and more like the person God created you to be is so encouraging. Each movement you make towards Christ is one step closer to living freely.

Memories of my childhood are slowly coming back and the emotional numbness is gone. The beautiful ending to this otherwise sad story is that now I have the emotional capacity to experience peace, joy, love, and God on a whole new level. I truly feel transformed.

Battling Powerfully (The Spiritual Pathway)
Chapter Nine

Refresh

For we are not unaware of the devil's schemes. 2 Corinthians 2:11

If we were to translate God's clear counsel in this verse into modern-day language, it would probably go something like: "Don't be stupid about what's really going on!" or "Don't be oblivious about what's in the dark!"

Much of the intention in *Soul Healing* is to demystify the reality of spiritual battle. To live the free, peace-filled lives we want, fighting an unseen enemy is a must. We can't be misled by the really crazy stuff out there. Being weirded out is just another scheme against us. Instead, let's grab hold of every one of the strategies in this chapter and put it in a toolbox labeled "Not Unwise of Evil Schemes" kit."

This subject is far from new. In the 1600s, Anglican-Puritan writer William Gurnall published *The Christian in Complete Armour.* It was one of the first books written on the subject of spiritual warfare. In it, the author stressed the importance of reading Scripture, prayer, and calling on the name of Christ for protection as well as to counteract the plans of the enemy. If Christians needed instruction back then on these matters, it's not surprising we are in even more need today.

Satan and the other fallen angels' purposes in attacking the human soul remain the same. The goals of these evil forces are to deceive humanity, thwart God's purposes, prevent unbelievers from placing faith in Christ, limit a Christian's power, and stop the Gospel from being spread. They seek to:

- hinder prayers (Daniel 10:12-13)
- cause sickness and disease (Matthew 9:32-33; Acts 10:37-38)
- blind the minds of humans (2 Corinthians 4:4)
- rule the world (Luke 4:7)
- steal the Word of God (Matthew 13:19)
- steal, kill, and destroy everything about believer's lives (John 10:10)
- plant doubt (Matthew 13:37-39)

Experienced any of those lately?

Let's fill up that toolbox!!

Reflect

How can you be healed by learning to focus on what is rather than what isn't?

And my God will meet all your needs according to His glorious riches in Christ Jesus.
Philippians 4:19

In what areas are you struggling with discontentment?

> Discontentment dries up the soul.
> Elisabeth Elliot

What comes to mind when you think about drenching—your whole body in the ocean or settling for an empty little Coke can?

Let the word of Christ dwell in you richly as you teach and admonish one another with all wisdom, and as you sing psalms, hymns and spiritual songs with gratitude in your hearts to God.
Colossians 3:16

> All earthly delights are but streams. But God is the ocean.
> Jonathan Edwards

> We will never be happy until we make God the source of our fulfillment and the answer to our longings.
> Stormie Omartian

What is your reaction to this quote: "Turning our attention away from God's hand and placing it on God's face will work to transform us every time"?

Think of some ways you might be missing God's love/provision/deliverance in your life.

Years ago, a young client was excited about her relationship with her boyfriend. They were starting to get serious after a bit of dating until one day when he didn't answer her calls. She came into her next session reporting he had been found dead in his apartment. He died from carbon monoxide poisoning. This was right around the time that carbon monoxide detectors were coming on the scene. We can only imagine the thousand "if onlys" that this girl and the boy's family experienced.

There is now no condemnation for those who are in Christ Jesus.
Romans 8:1

Carbon monoxide indicators let us know when something toxic is around even though we can't smell, see, or sense it. God has given us similar alarm systems to recognize spiritual onslaught. Shame, confusion, fear, doubt, hopelessness, powerlessness, insecurity, and condemnation are like these alarms. These are antithetical to the Word of God.

Therefore, when we as believers experience them, they alert us to the fact that something toxic is affecting us. It is so hard for us to realize that when we have such thoughts or feelings, it's time to fight! We are being signaled that there is something coming against us – we're being exposed to something that is poisoning our sanctified souls.

We demolish arguments and every pretension that sets itself up against the knowledge of God, and we take captive every thought to make it obedient to Christ.
2 Corinthians 10:5

Which of those "indicators" or "alarms" do I typically fall prey to and don't recognize as hell's lies taking root in me?

What does it mean that spiritual warfare is not a power encounter, but a truth encounter?

What new thought or perspective or "how to" for doing spiritual battle is God giving you?

How have you seen in your own life that making steps towards God will be opposed?

You, dear children, are from God and have overcome them, because the One who is in you is greater than the one who is in the world.
1 John 4:4

What are some lies that evil has been whispering (or shouting) to you today, or even in the past hour?

Submit yourselves, then, to God. Resist the devil, and he will flee from you.
James 4:7

When we begin to do daily life with the understanding that the battle is external to us, then victorious living is ours! It's outside of us – though in the realm of the spirit – and we must clearly envision it outward, not inward.

Because evil is constantly lying and our job is to be conscious and attentive to this battle, here is an excellent tool: before your head hits the pillow each night, write down at least one lie evil has tried to tell you that day. Keep a notepad by your bed or even on your pillow, and do not allow yourself to go to sleep without exposing at least one venomous arrow from your wicked adversary. Just doing that will help you become more skilled at fighting attack.

Spiritual practices enhance our ability to experience the full life Christ purchased for us. They do not get us "more" of God, as many mistakenly think. Instead, they allow us to more directly experience the Jesus now living in us, fully victorious, giving complete strength and freedom.

Explain these practices in your own words.

Experience God's presence:

Practice thankfulness:

"Be not afraid of saying too much in the praise of God; all the danger is of saying too little.

Matthew Henry"

"When thou has truly thanked the Lord for every blessing sent, but little time will then remain for murmur or lament.

Hannah More"

Hold death closely:

Give when and what you would like to receive:

Go on a God hunt:

"God is not a God that hides himself, but a God who made all that he might reveal himself.

George McDonald"

Of these, which one is God prompting you to pursue? What specifically will you do today to obey His prompting?

Recall a recent bad day or week you've had. In the left hand column, recount each "bad" event that happened.

Now, if you were looking for God, knowing that He was absolutely there with you, where would you have seen Him? Write these possibilities in the right hand column.

Events	Where I could've seen God
I woke up 20 minutes late.	*He woke me up! It could've been two hours late!*
I sped to work and was stopped by the police.	*I didn't get in an accident or hurt myself or anyone else.*
He gave me a $100 ticket.	*We have jobs which allow us to pay for this.*
My son's school called that afternoon; he was throwing up and needed to go home	*I have a flexible job which allows me to leave when my children are sick.*

Though the fig tree does not bud and there are no grapes on the vines, though the olive crop fails and the fields produce no food, though there are no sheep in the pen and no cattle in the stalls, yet I will rejoice in the Lord, I will be joyful in God my Savior. The sovereign Lord is my strength, he makes my feet like the feet of a deer, he enables me to go on the heights.
Habakkuk 3:17-19

How long, O Lord? Will you forget me forever? How long will you hide your face from me? How long must I wrestle with my thoughts and every day have sorrow in my heart? ... But I trust in your unfailing love; my heart rejoices in your salvation. I will sing to the Lord, for He has been good to me.
Psalm 13:1-2, 5-6

Then you will know the truth, and the truth will set you free.
John 8:32

Resolve

Put on the full armor of God so that you can take your stand against the devil's schemes. Ephesians 6:11

To counteract the deeds of foul spirits in the unseen world, God instructs us to wear spiritual armor. The full armor described in Ephesians 6:14-18 includes a belt, shield, breastplate, sandals, helmet and a sword. Just like we wouldn't think about fighting in a war without protection, Christians need to put on the armor every day since we are constantly being pummeled.

The armor of God is a covering of truth, righteousness, peace, faith, salvation, and the Word. Putting on the armor of God happens by prayer, reading Scripture, or during times of praise and worship. When we're "armored up," Christians have offensive and defensive weapons that will ward off attacks from hell's envoys.

When we use the tools from this chapter, we in fact do take a stand against evil's schemes. Donning the armor allows us to see what's really real. This chapter began with the verse: "For we are not unaware of the devil's schemes" (2 Corinthians 2:11). By God's grace, our understanding of hell's tactics and ploys become clear as we fight the battle, and as we do, vile spiritual rogues are enraged all the more. Again, Lewis depicts this well in *Screwtape Letters*. Here is his description of an evil spirit's response when a Christian has come to perceive what's really going on and the demonic is exposed:

"You have let a soul slip through your fingers... It makes me mad to think of it. How well I know what happened at the instant when they snatched him from you! There was a sudden clearing of his eyes (was there not?) as he saw you for the first time, and recognized the part you had had in him and knew that you had it no longer. Just think (and let it be the beginning of your agony) what he felt at that moment; as if a scab had fallen from an old sore, as if he were emerging from a hideous, shell-like tether, as if he shuffled off for good and all a defiled, wet, clinging garment."[14]

Praise be to our God, who unveils all truth!

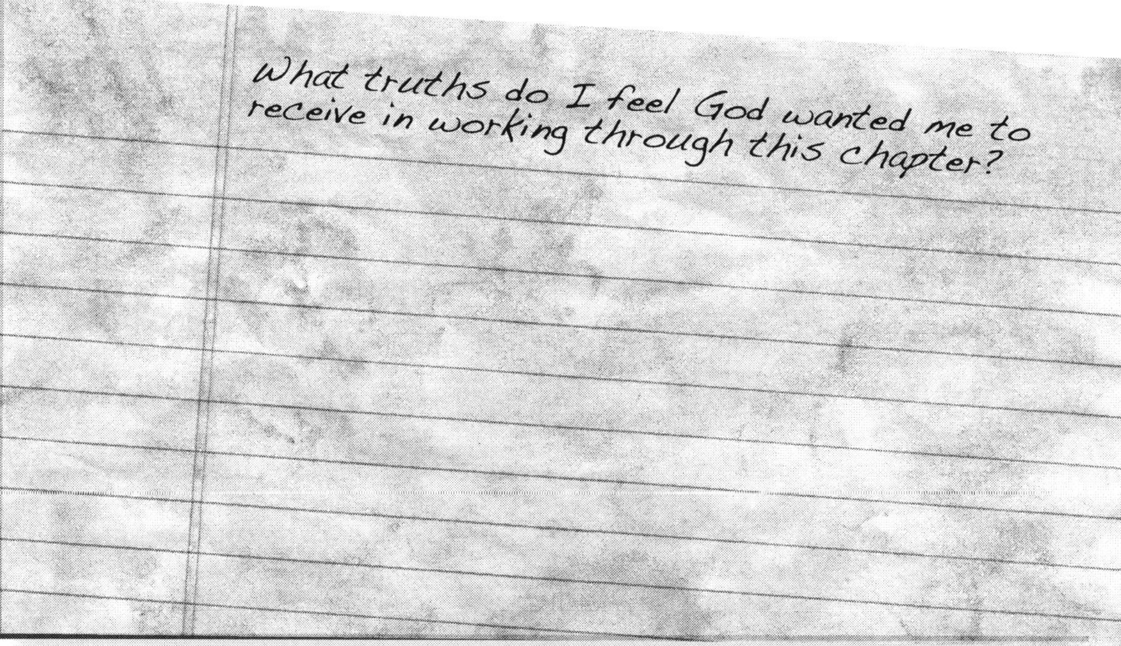

Making Change (The Behavioral Pathway)
Chapter Ten

Refresh
It's always interesting, and confirming, when in the midst of writing certain sections, God speaks a validating point through someone. It happened on the day of writing this present portion. Chapter 10 is focused on making behavioral changes to assist the full healing work of God to take root in our lives. Just this morning, a client spoke these words about his own process of behavioral adjustments:

"The only way to bring about change is to force yourself through it. Regardless of my feelings, I have to just keep trying. I just think - push through the awkwardness ten more times. I have to keep forcing myself through this."

This person knows how to recognize spiritual battle, stay on truth, and live free from the effects of past hurts. He was referring to actually living out the level of healing and maturity he now experiences in his soul. He is trying to make his external behavior line up with his internal reality.

Researchers claim simple repetitive tasks require a timeframe of around 21 days to condition. With the power of God pulsating through the believer, who knows what this timeframe is for a Christian! However, trying a new action 21 times before ever evaluating whether it is "working" is not a bad paradigm.

Though the strategies and tools in this chapter might seem cumbersome or clumsy at first, keep at them. It's a money-back guarantee that after awhile, if you keep at them, you will truly begin to behave and act in ways more true to the intended masterpiece God has designed you to be! Like wearing new clothes, give them time to break in. Sooner or later, you will begin to feel at home in that which once seemed foreign.

Reflect
Our "voice" is a part of God's image within us and is intended to be a powerful force for His work.

How do you understand this idea of "voice"?

Describe your understanding of what it means to "lose one's voice" as described on page 249.

What's an example of an appropriate use of voice?

An inappropriate one?

What is a wise use of voice for a Christian?

How have your hurts handicapped you when it comes to knowing what your needs are and how to appropriately express them?

Spend some time assessing:

Physically, what do I need right now?

Emotionally, what would benefit me?

What is missing in my spiritual life?

Intellectually, what do I need?

Instead, speaking the truth in love, we will in all things grow up into him who is the Head, that is, Christ.
Ephesians 4:15.

"Our neediness, properly handled, is a link to His presence.
Sarah Young"

Learning to speak all forms of truth with humility is a sign of growing up or maturing in Christ.

Which one of these phrases is most difficult for you to express? Why?

Would you please...?
I'd really like if... x
I like...
I wish...
I don't like...
Would you be willing to...?
Can you help me...?

this one because it feels selfish and Christians aren't supposed to be selfish

Larry Crabb identifies self-protection as sinful.[15] How would you describe self-protection?

Tammy describes it this way:
"Self-protective behavior in any form is hurtful. Upholding vows, anesthetizing oneself, wearing masks, and living in hiding relational patterns all stem from agreeing with evil that you have to take care of yourself. It's important to consider why this action is so very damaging. Ultimately, to do so is to say to God, 'You cannot be trusted.' Sure, we trust Him in many areas, but when it comes to the hurt in our hearts, and how desperately we don't want to feel that again, many of us take matters into our own hands. Seriously now, how many of us, even as Christians, live with our hearts barricaded? It just hurts too much to put ourselves out there again – to share insecure thoughts with a friend, to disclose an ugly habit to a mentor, to hope that our new friend will be loyal. Instead we serve and love and give···up to a point. Living free from the effects of our wounds also means demolishing this brick wall and refusing to keep our hearts hidden." (page 252)

In what ways have you self-protected in the past?

What is your reaction to the statement, "Hurt people hurt people"?

On page 253, Tammy says to put something "to bed forever" is to "deal with a lie and make a decision to cross the threshold and live in a new truth."

What do you, right now, need to put to bed forever?

Is there a lie that has so gripped you that you have felt powerless under it?
Is there bitterness you know lives on in your heart?
A mask that needs laid down?
A pattern of self protection of which you need to repent?
A habit stealing your freedom that you will stop?
A vow you must revoke?

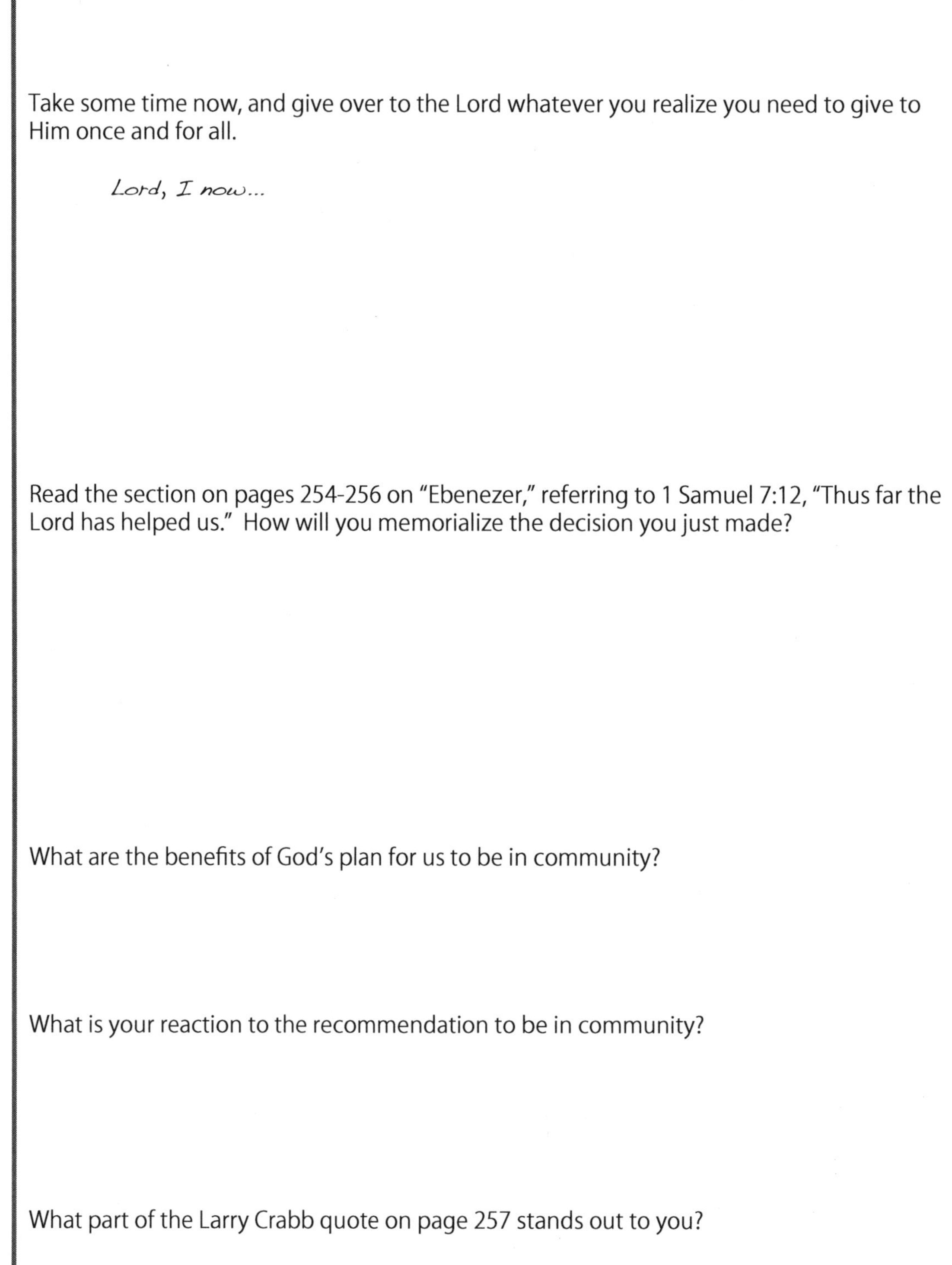

Take some time now, and give over to the Lord whatever you realize you need to give to Him once and for all.

Lord, I now...

Read the section on pages 254-256 on "Ebenezer," referring to 1 Samuel 7:12, "Thus far the Lord has helped us." How will you memorialize the decision you just made?

Let us not give up meeting together, as some are in the habit of doing, but let us encourage one another—and all the more as you see the Day approaching.
Hebrews 10:25

What are the benefits of God's plan for us to be in community?

What is your reaction to the recommendation to be in community?

What part of the Larry Crabb quote on page 257 stands out to you?

Name at least one person who "really knows your heart, goals, dreams, struggles, and joys?"

"To make changes in our behavior means we will need to 'try on' these new actions." (p. 261) Describe how that perspective is different from any previous assumptions you have made about how change happens.

What are some new behaviors, actions, attitudes, or perspectives you now need to "try on" as part of your healing process?

Reflect

We are forgetful people. We worry today about finances though we made it through last month when all looked bleak. We pray for strength to get through a conversation, only to freak out the next time we have to work through a conflict. It is incredibly challenging for the frail human mind to hold onto faith.

The skills given in this chapter are for that purpose alone – to congeal the healing changes God has wrought in your life. Tammy asks,

"Will you, when stuck, pull out this resource God has given you to go after whatever is getting in between you and true, close communion with your Father? This is, in a nutshell, the entire vision God gave me for this work."

True closeness, peace, joy, contentment, and intimacy with the Lord are yours! Now!! We must, however, set the table before we sit down to eat. That's what concepts like using your voice, laying down self-protection, being direct with needs and requests, cultivating community, and selecting Ebenezers do. Healthy behaviors provide appropriate rails on which a healing soul can glide.

> Sow an act, and you reap a habit. Sow a habit and you reap a character. Sow a character and you reap a destiny.
> Anonymous

Someone once said that happiness is a consequence of holiness. Insofar as holiness is a structured approach to behavioral choices that honor God, that statement is true. There is no happiness outside of a life connected to the Savior. *Soul Healing* is all about doing whatever necessary to remove any and all hindrances, schemes, and barriers in the way of a soul's connectedness to Jesus. Watch for your sense of joy as it increases in direct proportion to the holy choices you make.

You have come a long way on this intense journey. God is being glorified in your diligence and faithfulness. May you sense His deepest blessing on you for such obedience and perseverance.

Feeling Your Way (The Emotional Pathway)
Chapter Eleven

Refresh

The human soul undulates. Similar to a light wave, we have consistent and clear "ups" and "downs." Because we are emotional entities, in addition to being physical, spiritual, social, and intellectual ones, we undulate. Emotionally speaking, feelings will come and go. Highs and lows are a part of human existence. We would do well to actually come to expect this cyclical pattern in our lives.

However, being hurt or disappointed can cause people to try to protect from this natural undulation. In an attempt to control, they strive hard to cut out the bad or sad: to become impervious to hurt. In theory, that might seem like it works. But, when we cut off the bottom part of the undulating wave, the top part is cut off as well. The result is a very restricted range of emotion and experience.

God can't be contained within such a controlled range of emotional experience. Living with the highs and lows cut off was not His intention for us, but He often gets the blame when we just don't "feel" our connection to Him.

What the Lord offers is a level of peace, joy, and contentment that is unattainable through any other pursuit. A sense of satisfaction, of true rest, of fulfillment and comfort – these are the results of life hidden in Christ. 1 Peter 1:8 uses the phrase "joy inexpressible." Indeed, it is a depth of feeling unable to be expressed in human language when we are yielded, trusting, and moving in the Spirit of Jesus.

And, this too will undulate. That fact means absolutely nothing about your true connectedness to Christ. It simply means you are cycling, like we humans do. God hasn't moved. The Spirit hasn't "gone anywhere." It's possible that you might just be hungry... or tired... or hormonally annoyed. The point is that we cannot permit ourselves to draw conclusions about who God is in our emotional swings.

This chapter provides many tools for healthy emotional expression and ways of being. When we permit God to have full access to our emotional selves through mature practices, adult perspectives, and security-driven strategies, our feelings can be a great place of blessing and intimacy with the Lord. Even through our undulations.

He'll be faithful to you, though your heart is untrue, and your love's grown cold. His forgiveness is real. It'll comfort and heal your sin weary soul. Through all your years, your joy, your tears, He is all you need.

- Steve Camp

Reflect

What is something new or different about emotions that this chapter has made you consider?

Why does it not work to simply tell ourselves to stop thinking or feeling something? What's a good alternative?

> "Happiness depends on what happens; joy does not.
> Oswald Chambers"

> "A life lived in God is not lived on the plane of feelings, but of the will.
> Elisabeth Elliot."

"Becoming tolerant of the fact that certain issues will flare up occasionally does not mean that you are not healed. It merely validates that we have a schemer who knows our hurts and seeks to use those against us on a regular basis." Rewrite this idea in your own words.

Instead, speaking the truth in love, we will in all things grow up into him who is the Head, that is, Christ.
Ephesians 4:15.

Like being in an emotional gym, it helps to do "reps" to strengthen the muscles used in emotional expression. Do a few reps here, practicing how to identify and express what you are feeling:

I feel ____ because ______
Right now I feel ____
Today I felt mostly _______
The strongest emotion I've had lately was _______

Why is saying "You make me feel..." not wise?

What vulnerable areas in my soul might I need to warn those who love me about?

Can you think of some Scriptural examples of bringing your strongest emotions to God?

What does the fact that all the Psalms were used in worship say to you about your emotions?

Identify an emotion you have had today and talk to God about it.

Lord, it's hard for me to slow down to even know what I feel sometimes, but I know earlier I was feeling discouraged about my parenting, my marriage, our finances... but I now see that I was just listening to lies.

You know how sad I get when I compare myself to my friends...

The sacrifices of God are a broken spirit; a broken and contrite heart, O God, you will not despise.
Psalm 51:17

What comes to your mind when you think of brokenness? What are some ideas about brokenness found on page 279?

"True healing cannot come without emptying oneself of the natural and insidious pride every human has. Wounded or not, every one of us has a significant regard for self – think of how we gauge every situation through the lens of how it will affect us, how well we keep ourselves fed and clothed, and how we somehow find the time to watch the shows we want. The point is that our natural bent is not towards brokenness and authenticity. We must exert our will to put ourselves in that posture intentionally, lest we be forced there." (page 280)

How is God speaking to you about your own level of brokenness or pride?

Your strongest or most distinct memories hold keys to when lies became implanted, vows were made, or schemes were unleashed. Even if at first blush you might think, "That was no big deal," if it's vivid, it is that way for a reason. The Spirit is very merciful to give us clues through these.

What are a few of your most intense memories?

What is the Lord revealing to you about them?

Resolve

As God has ministered to you through the exploration of memories and emotion, consider this passage in *Legacy of the Heart: The Spiritual Advantages of a Painful Childhood* by Wayne Muller:

"Each childhood wound and every spiritual teaching has been presented to help us cultivate a particular aspect of mercy and compassion toward ourselves. At each juncture we have been confronted with a choice: Do we meet ourselves and our wounds with judgment or with mercy? Do we touch our childhood memories with anger, or soften them with love and forgiveness? Do we recall our violations with shame or embrace them with genuine acceptance; do we react with fear and isolation or with faith and courage? Do we add to the violence within ourselves, or do we cultivate unconditional love and kindness for all we have been and all we have become?"[16]

Two of my good friends had allowed God to take hold of their hearts, soften them, and shore up their marriage. After years together, they were approaching middle-age and decided to see if God would bless their changed hearts with a child. He did. These two deeply beloved people were saturated in excitement and thrill over their coming addition. Then, at week twenty, everything changed. The doctor sadly informed them that their daughter had a genetic condition and would not survive. Certainly, secular medical approach recommended procedures to end the pregnancy immediately.

Because such a scenario is unimaginable except for those to whom it has happened, what is imaginable is the gamut of emotions they had. This was certainly true of my friends. And their emotions were magnified because they decided to wait. And wait. And wait. Even when fluids were so low as to indicate certain death, her little heart kept beating. By the seventh and eighth weekly appointments past the doctor's longest guess for when she would die, he was at a loss for words. Sixteen weeks in all did my friends wait in excruciating pain and grief until their daughter was dancing with Jesus.

As we waited in the hospital for Abigail's body to be delivered, it was perhaps the worst of all. No one was delivering balloons or flowers, and there was a special apparent "loss inside" mark on their door. Yet inside, an entirely unexpected event was transpiring. Unexpected, that is, to the medical staff who did not know the Lord. To those that were His, it was very clear what was going on.

In the wee hours of the morning, her tiny little shell had come. A small band of us gathered around the bed as the doctor laid her body, wrapped in a crocheted purple blanket, in my friends' arms. We looked; we cried; we hugged. We read God's Word and talked about how her life had touched so many people, though she had never taken a breath on this earth. And we were squeezed in a tight little "Christian circle" that included the medical personnel, clearly taking it all in. At one point, the doctor looked at me and said, "It's not usually like this. No one's ever happy, and usually the couple is all alone."

It was in the middle of this scene that my friend, Abigail's mother, looked up with puzzlement and calm as she held her daughter's still body. Her big brown eyes were full, and she said, "I have peace." She nodded as though to confirm her own statement, and repeated it again with bewilderment and amazement, "I have peace."

To think that a woman could hold the dead body of her only child and have peace exude from her every pore would seem ludicrous. Yet, this is the true reality for everyone who allows Christ's presence into every nook and cranny of their undulating hearts.

Since that time, I've come to refer to this as the "peace that doesn't make sense." It is based on Philippians 4:7:

"...and the peace of God, which transcends all understanding, will guard your hearts and minds in Christ Jesus."

When we allow our emotional selves to be openly and fully communing with God through His Spirit within, we, too, can experience a peace that makes no sense given our circumstances, situations, or setbacks.

Real Healing

Real-life testimonies of people on the Soul Healing Journey

Amy's Story

In some ways I don't know where to begin, but really I know exactly where to begin: with Abigail. November 18, 2008 is a day that changed us forever. We were at our routine 20 week ultrasound with our doctor, but it turned out to be not so routine. The doctor told us that we were having a girl, but that our baby had triploidy, which meant that she had three sets of every chromosome instead of two. We were stunned to hear that she could not live outside the womb. We named our daughter Abigail, which means, "Father's joy."

According to the doctor, Abigail shouldn't have lived past 28 weeks gestation, but her little heart continued beating until week 36. For 16 weeks, we went to see Abigail and see her heartbeat on the ultrasound. On March 6, 2009 at 10:59pm, Abigail's little 1 pound 8 ounce, 14 inch long body was delivered. If someone had told me what that night was going to be like, I wouldn't have believed them. I cannot even begin to explain what an amazing sense of peace and joy we experienced that night! Yes, we had joy! Our daughter was dead and we were joyful. How is that even possible? Only God, that's how.

God's spirit was all over the room that night. My husband was transformed. I don't even have words to describe Billy that night. I do know that he was such a proud daddy! If he could have, he would have shown off his sweet little girl to everyone he knew, and even those he didn't know. Only God, our amazing, gracious, merciful and loving God, could have taken something so sad and made it so good. And it was *so good.*

Do I still have peace and joy when it comes to Abigail? Yes. Do I wish she were here with me today? Yes. Would I have chosen this journey for myself? No. Would I change anything about this journey? No.

That may sound crazy, but I wouldn't change a thing. The only reason I can say that is because of Jesus. I am so thankful for Abigail and I am so thankful for what God has taught me through her. I know His ways are better than mine. I know the fact that Abigail is with Jesus and not with me is for my own good, so that God can continue a good work in me for HIS GLORY. The journey has not been easy. It has been hard, lonely, painful, and sad. But because of this journey, I KNOW Jesus. I know what it is like to walk through the valley of the shadow of death and to be held every step of the way by Jesus. I know Him in a way I would have never known Him had Abigail not died.

Abigail made me uncomfortable with life here on earth. That is a good thing, because really, I should be uncomfortable. This is not my home. I really don't belong here. My home is with my daughter, and with Jesus, in heaven.

As I write this, I woke up this morning feeling sad, missing Abigail. Then I realized that she would have been five months old today. So, where am I today, five months later? Uncomfortable, but hopeful. I know beyond a shadow of a doubt that God loves me and is faithful to me. I trust Him. Psalm 31:14-15 says, *"I trust in you. O Lord; I say you are my God. My times are in your hands."* So, I eagerly await our future with a peace that transcends all understanding. (Phil:4:7). Thank you, Jesus.

What truths do I feel God wanted me to receive in
working through this chapter?

A Better Life
Chapter Twelve

Refresh

At this stage in such a well-done journey, allow your heart to pause a moment and be refreshed by these Scriptures:

"He has sent me to bind up the brokenhearted, to proclaim freedom for the captives and release from darkness for the prisoners,
To proclaim the year of the Lord's favor and the day of vengeance of our God,
To comfort all who mourn, and provide for those who grieve in Zion –
To bestow on them a crown of beauty instead of ashes, the oil of gladness instead of mourning, and a garment of praise instead of a spirit of despair.
They will be called oaks of righteousness, a planting of the Lord for the display of this splendor.
They will rebuild the ancient ruins and restore the places long devastated; they will renew the ruined cities that have been devastated for generations." Isaiah 61:1-4

"The Lord will surely comfort Zion and will look with compassion on all her ruins; he will make her deserts like Eden, her wastelands like the garden of the Lord. Joy and gladness will be found in her, thanksgiving and the sound of singing." Isaiah 51:3

"The ransomed of the Lord will return. They will enter Zion with singing; everlasting joy will crown their heads. Gladness and joy will overtake them, and sorrow and sighing will flee away." Isaiah 51:11

"The desert and the parched land will be glad; the wilderness will rejoice and blossom." Isaiah 35:1

Ahhh, do you hear it? Do you sense the Spirit's comfort and hope? Can you see plainly the plan of God for the hard and hurting areas of your heart?

Evil wants us to believe that the places in our souls marked by devastation will always be dead and gone. Hell itself is countering a massive offensive to tempt us to believe that the wastelands in the aftermath of painful experiences will be filled with garbage forever; that our rejection, betrayal, emotional damage, physical abuse, infidelity, or abandonment will never be redeemed. And at times, it is challenging for us to believe anything could ever grow in such hard places again.

God promised water in the desert and blossoms in the wilderness. Jesus said beauty would come from ashes and that praise would replace despair. Isaiah said sorrow and sighing would be no more as deserts become lush and garbage dumps become garden paradise. Such hope is alive for us today. By calling Jesus Christ out from a cold dark tomb, God proved beyond doubt His ability to fulfill these promise.

Please, continue to allow the Holy Spirit into your desolation; then watch carefully. With eyes of faith, determinedly see how today is just a bit different from yesterday or last month. Sprouts will appear in your wastelands. You can count on it. Little by little, He will work His grace, transforming the barren places into fertile ground in which God's Word can take root, grow, and produce a bountiful harvest.
Yes, God has promised us hope and healing for all the barren places in our lives.

Do you believe that what is to come will be better than what has been?

Reflect

Until now, what about your life have you had a hard time embracing?

> "Crisis brings us face to face with our inadequacy and our inadequacy in turn leads us to the inexhaustible sufficiency of God.
>
> Catherine Marshall."

With eyes of faith, do you see at least one way God could turn this around and make it a way for blessing?

You intended to harm me, but God intended it for good to accomplish what is now being done, the saving of many lives.
Genesis 50:20

In what ways have you bowed down in your past?

Write your prayer in response to this question (page 295): "Will you and I apply the force of our will to faith – a faith that grabs hold of hurtful times and squeezes them until the good starts to drip out?"

> "There is something about having endured great loss that brings purity of purpose and strength in character.
>
> Barbara Johnson"

Real Healing

Real-life testimonies of people on the Soul Healing Journey

Wendy's Story

I sat in the middle of a room of women while miscarrying my precious baby. It was my second miscarriage in three months. I was asked to share how I was feeling with the group. What should I say?

During and after the first miscarriage, I went through a number of weeks in deep despair. A week and a half after that first miscarriage, my husband and I were scheduled to go on a vacation to the Grand Canyon. I didn't want to go. I was wallowing in my sadness and couldn't think of having fun with my husband or missing our three year old daughter, who was my biggest distraction, and usually the only reason I could get myself out of bed in the morning. Caring for her kept my mind off my pain. But God knew this time away from her and from the world was exactly what I needed. He met me on that trip in the desert in ways I haven't even been able to put into words. First Peter talks about a "joy inexpressible," and that's exactly what He filled me with that week. I came home healed and at peace.

But a few weeks later, a friend of mine announced that she was pregnant. It was a big blow, and I took it hard, grieving my loss and thinking about what could have been. But because Jesus was so close this time, I was able to turn my eyes right back to Him and within a few hours, after much prayer and journaling, I could say, through tears, "Okay, Lord, I trust You. Even if we never have another baby, I trust that You love me and have my best and my family's best firmly in Your mind. I choose to trust You." I remember thinking that victory was in this quick turning. I was so thankful that the Lord swiftly moved me through that despair and returned my eyes back to Him, filling me with peace once again.

Two days later, we learned that we were expecting again! I can't even tell you how overjoyed I was. But within three weeks, I started spotting. Then the spotting turned to heavy bleeding. I knew before even seeing the doctor what was happening. I was miscarrying again.

So there I sat, in a meeting, in the middle of a room of women, with my heart ripped in two as I lost my baby. I was devastated, hurt, and grieving, and yet, when faced with the opportunity to share with these women how I was feeling, all I wanted to do was praise the Lord! More than anything else, I wanted to give Him glory in this time of great pain. Even now, recalling that moment, it blows my mind! When I compared where I had been emotionally three months earlier, faced with the same sad situation, to where I was this time, I was completely amazed, and so grateful. Jesus had never been closer. Despite my circumstances, I was filled with His peace—a peace that truly passes understanding. By the world's standards, I shouldn't have been feeling this way, two days after beginning a miscarriage. And the enemy would love for me to be depressed, turning inward, dwelling on my sadness and not wanting me to talk to anyone (like I did after the first miscarriage). Trust me, there was a piece of me that really wanted to hide, curled up in a ball in tears, but in His strength, I chose instead to walk in His peace and victory and the joy of the Lord. More than any other truth, He showed me through these miscarriages that <u>He</u> is my hope, not a baby, or anything or anyone else.
Thank you, Jesus.

What biblical examples or principles or passages or even examples from others' lives can you think of which speak to this?

Resolve

> "I will be found by you," declares the Lord, "and will bring you back from captivity. I will gather you from all the nations and places where I have banished you."
> Jeremiah 29:14
>
> The Jews in captivity would be restored back to what they had lost – the land of Promise. That's always the way of God for those who seek Him. Job, after all his troubles, was given double what he'd lost because he clung to God and never let go. Joseph was made doubly fruitful in the land of his affliction because he never lost sight of the God who was always with him, even in Egypt. When God's people lost what they were promised – whether through their own sin or someone else's – and continue to seek Him where He may be found, the result is always better than at first. God's abundance never decreases the second time around.
>
> The best is yet to come. That's how we are to live in this world: as citizens of what's yet to come. There is no grief, no sin, no problem, no frustration, no captivity, no abuse that cannot be redeemed and the redemption will be more than worthwhile. Paul assured us that the glory to be revealed will far outweigh anything in our present circumstances; that no eye has seen or ear heard what God has in store for those who love Him (1 Corinthians 2:9). We're to live like we know that.
>
> Chris Tiegreen[17]

What truths do I feel God wanted me to receive in working through this chapter?

You Go!
Chapter Thirteen

Refresh
In a society like ours, marked by exponential instant gratification, if you have journeyed this far, you are truly amazing! There are numbers of people that have started *Soul Healing* or this study guide, only to fall prey to some untruth about the work being too hard or too much. Praise God for your diligence and perseverance! Glory to Him that you know you are healed in Him, and now walk in that truth!

> Be much with the solid teachings of God's word... They shall produce in you a Christ-likeness at which the world shall stand astonished.
> Charles Spurgeon ”

It is true, whether you feel it or not, that you are changed from having taken this journey. We can't be under and exposed to this much Truth without being changed. If it's raining, and we're in the room, we are bound to get wet!! Thanks be to God that your life here forward will be forever different.

And we, who with unveiled faces all reflect the Lord's glory, are being transformed into his likeness with ever-increasing glory, which comes from the Lord, who is the Spirit.
2 Corinthians 3:18

Reflect
Of the three things that Tammy says that tend to grow us up (on page 297), which of those has been the impetus for the most change in your life? Why?

What are some characteristics of a person walking in the fullness of Christ's healing?

Which of these characteristics or perspectives do you thank God that exist in your own life?

By contrast, which of these characteristics or perspectives will you be asking God to help build and refine in you more and more?

Reread pages 302-307 and:

1. name someone to whom you need to stop comparing yourself forever:

and

2. name what some of your keys are:

One of the ways to overcome our culture's "the grass is always greener on the other side" mentality is to consistently choose contentment, thankfulness, and gratitude for the life God has given us, including everyone and everything in it. Instead of focusing on what is missing or that others have, list here as many of God's blessings to you as you can think of.

The new practices and perspectives included in this chapter are ones that take some time to form, but because they are God's will for your life, they will form, of that you can be sure. So, when thinking about changing from an immature to mature way of living, it's helpful to picture a marble and a chute analogy.

Our old behaviors have come about from wounds, circumstances, and situations that make up our personal past history. We have knee-jerk ways of reacting, typical patterns of thinking, and predictable behaviors. These are like chutes carved out inside of us. Each time there's a situation that is familiar, it's as if a marble is sent rolling down this chute, cueing us to our "typical" way of coping. With each marble, the chute becomes even more well-worn.

Well, in developing new behaviors, we are working to carve new "chutes." We want to form new ways of responding and reacting, based in God's truth. With each time we choose the new behavior or make the godly choice, we whittle away a little more on that chute in progress. Over time, the chute becomes fully functioning and successfully replaces the old. In the meantime, we'll try new actions and attitude, only to feel they fall short. They have! The new chute isn't finished yet. We can't be discouraged because change isn't instantaneous. Instead, have faith that with each legitimate try at a godly habit, you are reworking internal programming that kept you insecure, guarded, or trapped and soon you will be experiencing true freedom!

Also, this analogy can help us understand why it seems going backwards comes so quickly, or easily. It's only because these former grooves were well-worn. Take heart – soon they will be shut down forever. But in the meantime, keep whittling!

What is a new thought of maturity that God has shown you through this study?

What will victory in my major struggles look like?

What is victory in Christ?

Resolve

The last three headings in the chapter frame up a good reminder for us as we carry our new tools into everyday life:

Victory is in the process
Change takes time
Stay the course

We have to shed our instant-gratification, wow-me-with-razzle-dazzle cultural lens, and instead look and listen through the still, small, steady, and sure movement of the Spirit. He is there. He is working. He is faithful to you. His transformation touches every area of our lives, from our skin and bones to the deepest corner of our psyche. He is methodically restoring His image in us, an image straight from God Himself, not a result of will-power or self-improvement.

We do well to remember: "Victorious living is not an instant arrival. It is the pursuit of one victorious day at a time until the sun sets on enough to begin forming victorious habits."[18]

And here is our mandate:

"Forget the former things; do not dwell on the past. See, I am doing a new thing! Now it springs up; do you not perceive it? I am making a way in the desert and streams in the wasteland." Isaiah 43:18-19

Forge ahead beyond your hurts. Do not obsess over what you cannot undo. Believe God is doing something great. Look for it. Search yourself and see hope appear where it was not. Look for strength where there was none. See specks of joy eking through from shards of previous pain.

It's all about what we're looking for. Our clearest vision is through the habitual discipline of looking for Him. By faith, scan the horizon of your soul, take stock of your behavior, and be mindful of your inner dialogues. You will see Him. You must only keep looking for Him. He is not a God who hides Himself. He promises, "I will be found by you."

"You will seek me and find me when you seek me with all your heart. I will be found by you," declares the Lord, "and will bring you back from captivity."
Jeremiah 29:13-14a

And as a final encouragement to keep our sight on Him no matter what, here are words from a wise saint:

"O my soul, thou hast not one single promise only, like Abraham, but a thousand promises, and many patterns of faithful believers before thee: it behooves thee, therefore, to rely with confidence upon the Word of God. And though He delayeth His help, and the evil seemeth to grow worse and worse, be not weak but rather strong, and rejoice, since the most glorious promises of God are generally fulfilled in such a wondrous manner that He steps forth to save us at a time when there is the least appearance of it.

He commonly brings His help in our greatest extremity, that His finger may plainly appear in our deliverance. And this method He chooses that we may not trust upon anything that we see or feel, as we are always apt to do, but only upon His bare Word, which we may depend upon in every state."

C. H. Von Bogatzky[19]

Precious *Soul Healing* friend, ***keep looking for Him!!!***

What truths do I feel God wanted me to receive in working through this chapter?

Christ in you, the hope of glory. Colossians 1:27

This truth is where we begin and end. As a believer in Christ, His life now resides in you. He is the perfect and absolute definition of beauty. God has made you in His image – a masterpiece of His hands – and then indwelt your spirit through faith. Awe-inspiring, to be sure!

Yet, many Christians wrongly struggle to receive more of Christ or His Spirit or even His presence. This is a major misperception which has many Christians perplexed, and figuratively chasing their tails to find "more of Jesus."

We already have the One we so earnestly want and desperately need. Then, what of this tension? The answer is that we don't need "more of Jesus;" we need less of ourselves. Only then will our perception of Him be more accurate and our apprehension of Him be more palpable.

You are the light of the world. A bright, glowing candle of pure light. The shade around you has become encrusted with layers of dirt and grime. Years of lies you believed, scars from childhood wounds, unforgiveness, sinful habits, self-protective vows, pursuit of comforts and idols···all of it built up until the flame was barely visible. The Light within was (and is) as bright as ever, but when the surrounding globe permits clinging filth, the light seems very dim. The bottom line is this -- if the dirt is tolerated, the light is occluded. Erode the muck, and the light will shine brightly.

We, who with unveiled faces all reflect the Lord's glory, are being transformed into his likeness with ever-increasing glory. 2 Corinthians 3:18

The incredible journey you have taken through this study guide has equipped you with all sorts of grime-removing implements. Your soul healing work has provided you with figurative wipes, rags, sprays, and cleaners for allowing the amazing light within you to be seen. Every time you recognize a lie, reject an evil arrow, refuse to put on a mask, express an appropriate emotion, choose a mature behavior over an immature one, risk loving another, identify a way you are reaching for false substitutes, grieve healthily over honest losses, engage God persistently in prayer, deny self's cry for constant satiation, read God's Word instead of giving into worldly pulls···any and every time you do any of these things, you are appropriating His cleansing power!!! Light shines brilliantly and beautifully through clear glass.

It is for freedom that Christ has set us free. Stand firm, then, and do not let yourselves be burdened again by a yoke of slavery. Galatians 5:1

When this happens, not only will the world see God more clearly through His masterwork of you, you will also be able to perceive His residence within you more evidently. The clarity is two-way! Therefore, you need not strive for more of God. Believer in Christ, you have Him already. The living, breathing Spirit of Jesus fully occupies every heart of faith. As you let God gently remove the barriers brought by hurt, discouragement, misplaced hopes, ungodly desires, and the deceptions the enemy has lodged in your heart, your capability to experience His indwelling presence will increase. As you persistently continue this good work God has begun, watch and listen as your soul settles into a newness of freedom, faith, peace, and love. These will come in increasing measure as you vigilantly keep watch over any hindrance to your communion with Jesus.[20]

"Turn your eyes upon Jesus" is not just a catchy phrase. It's a life-altering practice and what the journey of *Soul Healing* is intended to provide – a satisfying, exciting, intimate, and empowering experience of your true connectedness to the Lord. Though the following hymn was written about turning our eyes on Jesus and all else becoming dim, it's clear that the writer was not referring to eyesight and externals. She was blind. She knew that whenever we focus the attention of our souls on the fullness of Jesus Christ, nothing else compares. Let the blind woman's words wash over your healing heart in true worship:

O soul, are you weary and troubled?
No light in the darkness you see?
There's a light for a look at the Savior,
And life more abundant and free!

Turn your eyes upon Jesus,
Look full in His wonderful face,
And the things of earth will grow strangely dim,
In the light of His glory and grace.

Through death into life everlasting
He passed, and we follow Him there;
Over us sin no more hath dominion—
For more than conquerors we are!

Turn your eyes upon Jesus,
Look full in His wonderful face,
And the things of earth will grow strangely dim,
In the light of His glory and grace.

His Word shall not fail you—He promised;
Believe Him, and all will be well:
Then go to a world that is dying,
His perfect salvation to tell!

Turn your eyes upon Jesus,
Look full in His wonderful face,
And the things of earth will grow strangely dim,
In the light of His glory and grace.[21]

As I finish this study guide, I am most excited about...

The one who calls you is faithful and He will do it.
1 Thessalonians 5:24

When I complete this study guide, I am committing to...

End Notes

1. *Chris Tiegreen, "Resurrection Life," One Year Walk with God Devotional: 365 Daily Bible Readings to Transform Your Mind. (Carol Stream, IL: Tyndale House Publishers, Inc., 2004), p. 47.*
2. *Christ Tiegreen, "The Exchange of Grace," One Year Walk with God Devotional: 365 Daily Bible Readings to Transform Your Mind. (Carol Stream, IL: Tyndale House Publishers, Inc., 2004), p. 46.*
3. *Paul Levin, The New Birth. Retrieved September 25, 2009, from http://www.familynet-international.org/newbirth.htm.*
4. *Neil Anderson, Living Free in Christ. (Ventura, CA: Regal Books, 1993).*
5. *Rev. E. Vincent Ford, Becoming Prepared Spiritually, Mentally and Emotionally For The End Times. Retrieved September 25, 2009 from http://www.endtimespreparation.com.*
6. *Dan B. Allender, The Healing Path. (Colorado Springs, Colorado: Water Brook Press, 1999), p. 6.*
7. *Ibid., p. 6.*
8. *Ibid., p. xi.*
9. *C.S. Lewis, The Screwtape Letters. (New York: Touchstone, 1996), p. 54.*
10. *Ibid., p. 57.*
11. *Chris Tiegreen, Worship the King. (Carol Stream, IL: Tyndale House Publishers, Inc., 2008), September 10.*
12. *Ibid..*
13. *Sarah Young, Dear Jesus. (Nashville, TN: Thomas Nelson, 2007), p. 52-53.*
14. *C.S. Lewis, The Screwtape Letters. (New York: Touchstone, 1996), p. 109.*
15. *Larry Crabb, Inside Out. (Colorado Springs, CO: NavPress, 1988).*
16. *Wayne Muller, Legacy of the Heart: The Spiritual Advantages of a Painful Childhood, as cited in Marilyn Barrack, Soul Reflections: Many Lives, Many Journeys. (Corwin Springs, MT: Summit University Press, 2003), p. 90.*
17. *Chris Tiegreen, Worship the King. (Carol Stream, IL: Tyndale House Publishers, Inc., 2008), September 13.*
18. *Beth Moore, Praying God's Word. (Nashville, TN: B&H Books, 2000), p 152.*
19. *C.H. Von Bogatzky, "November 10," Streams in the Desert. (Grand Rapids, MI: Zondervan, 1997), p. 422-423.*
20. *Chris Tiegreen, Worship the King. (Carol Stream, IL: Tyndale House Publishers, Inc., 2008), September 11.*
21. *Helen H. Lemmel, Turn Your Eyes Upon Jesus. (1922). Retrieved September 30, 2009 from http://library.timelesstruths.org/music/Turn_Your_Eyes_upon_Jesus/htm.*

Notes